Tricia Milan

John Lowrie Morrison:

foreword by Rosalind Jones

the Colour of life

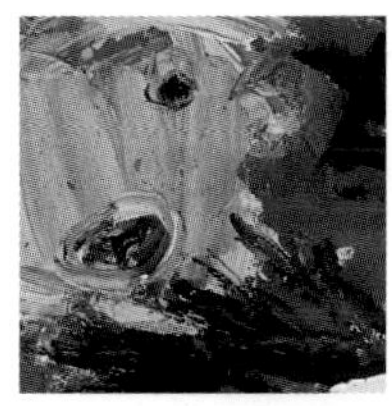

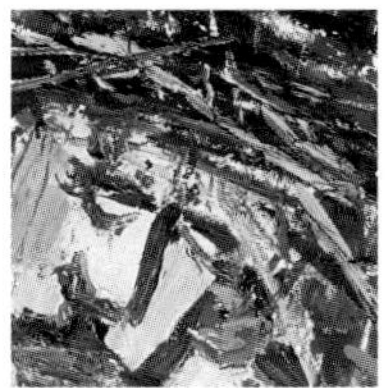

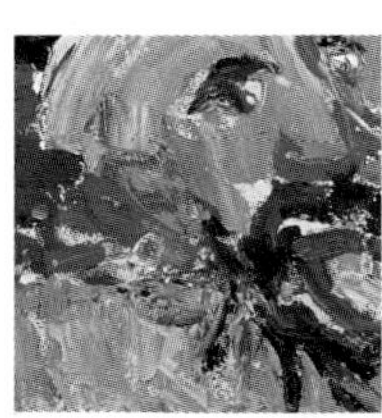
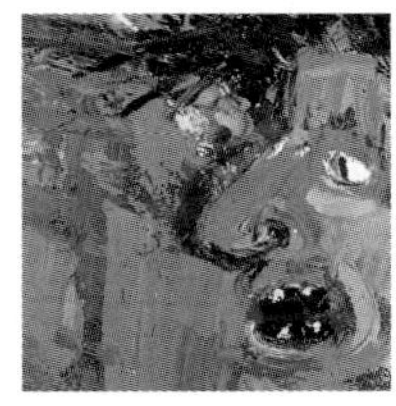

PUBLISHED BY SCOTTISH CHRISTIAN PRESS

First published in Great Britain
in 2002 by Scottish Christian Press
21 Young Street
Edinburgh
EH2 4HU

ISBN 1904325041

Cover design and layout Heather Macpherson
Printed and bound by Bath Press

John Lowrie Morrison and Rosalind Jones have asserted their right under the Copyright, Designs and Patents Act 1988, to be identified as Authors of this work.

Credits

B&W Studio Photography - David Ferguson
Colour Plate Photography - George Birrell

The publisher acknowledges subsidy from the Scottish Arts Council towards the publication of this volume.

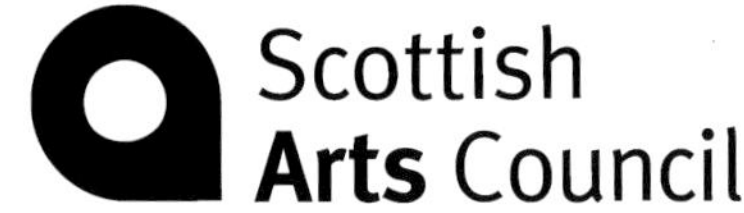

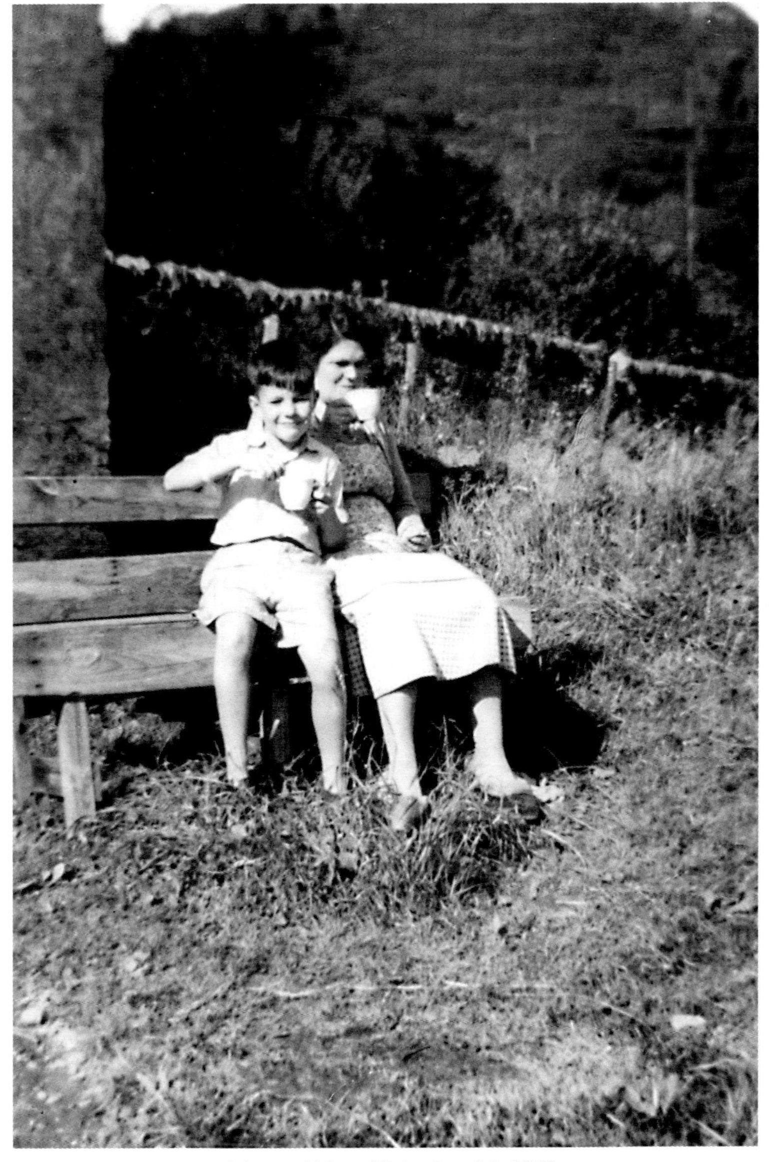

John and Mum, Tighnabruaich 1955

In loving memory of Bessie Alice Morrison (1915 - 2002)

Preface: on behalf of
The Princess Royal Trust for Carers

The question was simply asked: would you donate one of your paintings to a major auction we are holding as part of our 10th Anniversary celebrations? The answer in this case was: 'with pleasure'. Thus started the unique relationship between The Princess Royal Trust for Carers (PRTC) and John Lowrie Morrison.

Whether as the result of an exhibition of his paintings in a fashionable London gallery or an exhibition as part of an Hebridean cruise, Jolomo has pledged ongoing support to PRTC, which now includes the donation of royalties from sales of this book, *The Colour of Life*. The PRTC owes a debt of gratitude to John Lowrie Morrison and to Rosalind Jones, author of the foreword, who has similarly donated her royalty.

It is not just John's giving but the manner of it: quiet and dignified, with no fanfares or beating of drums. John and his wife Maureen are long-term carers themselves. They know at first hand the issues involved and have lived through them. But: who *is* a carer, and how can The Princess Royal Trust for Carers help?

Where do you turn when you hear some of the worst news that you can imagine? Your husband or wife is terminally ill and needs constant care; your son or daughter survives a car crash but is wheelchair bound for life; your aged parent is diagnosed with worsening dementia. The medical and technical help has done its part, and your loved one comes home. They need your constant attention. You are trying to juggle a job and the rest of the family with their specific needs. You're short of time, short of cash, short of expertise. On top of that, you're exhausted, stressed and worried. So, what now?

This is the situation which brought The Princess Royal Trust for Carers into being. The Trust is the first point of call for those people who find themselves in the position of caring for a friend or loved one. It helps carers to sort through the cluster of problems which they will be facing. Do they need professional advice from the social and health services? Are they entitled to any extra benefits? Will they need to give up their job? Should they move, or adapt their house? What about the rest of their family? How are they coping emotionally?

The PRTC works to reach carers, and develop services for them, across the country . There are now 119 Carers Centres throughout the UK including 29 Centres in Scotland. Each Carers Centre works to provide local services, which include everything from a simple listening ear and information, to personal support, access to respite care or practical help in the home, advocacy with social services and other service providers, and of course arranging training, social and recreational events for carers. A very important task is in helping to combat the isolation of carers and to ensure that no carer reaches crisis-point before they get the support they need to make it easier to cope.

So much of John Lowrie Morrison's work reflects the sense of serenity and peace that is important to carers especially during those quiet moments when the burden of caring is temporarily lifted. The Princess Royal Trust for Carers is indeed fortunate to have the support of this caring artist.

Mike Wheatley
Glasgow Autumn 2002

The Princess Royal Trust
for Carers
10 Years of Caring

Unlike many other Trusts, The PRTC raises all its income from fund-raising activities to ensure the growth of its network and achievement of its long term goals. Whether you are seeking help for yourself or a friend, or wish to make a donation, contact:

The Princess Royal Trust
for Carers
Campbell House
215 West Campbell Street
Glasgow G2 4TT
tel: 0141 221 5966,
fax: 0141 221 4623
email:
infoscotland@carers.org
www.carers.org

Registered Charity No.
SCO15975

a biography

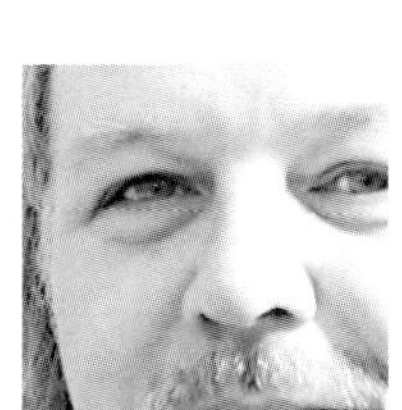

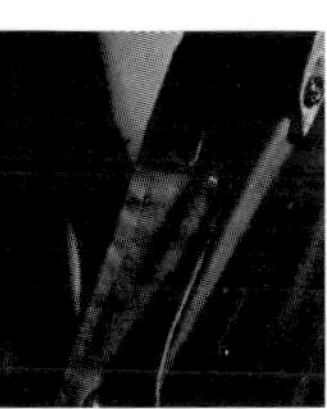

As a two year-old being bathed in the kitchen sink John Lowrie Morrison remembers creating his first drawing. The kitchen of the top floor tenement in Glasgow's Maryhill was steamy, and the window misted with condensation. While his mother soaped him he reached out a finger and doodled, fascinated by the tiny droplets on the cold, grey pane. Astonished at the sudden clarity of the marks he'd created he gazed through them to the world outside. Below in the side street he could see children playing, but the urban scene was dull and drab. Looking upwards the high-pitched, soot-spattered roof of the neighbouring tenement almost filled his view, but peering higher still he discovered a wedge of bright blue sky. Between the grey rooftops he saw colour and light that contrasted dramatically with the dingy city below. This earliest childhood memory is symbolic of the life and work of the artist today.

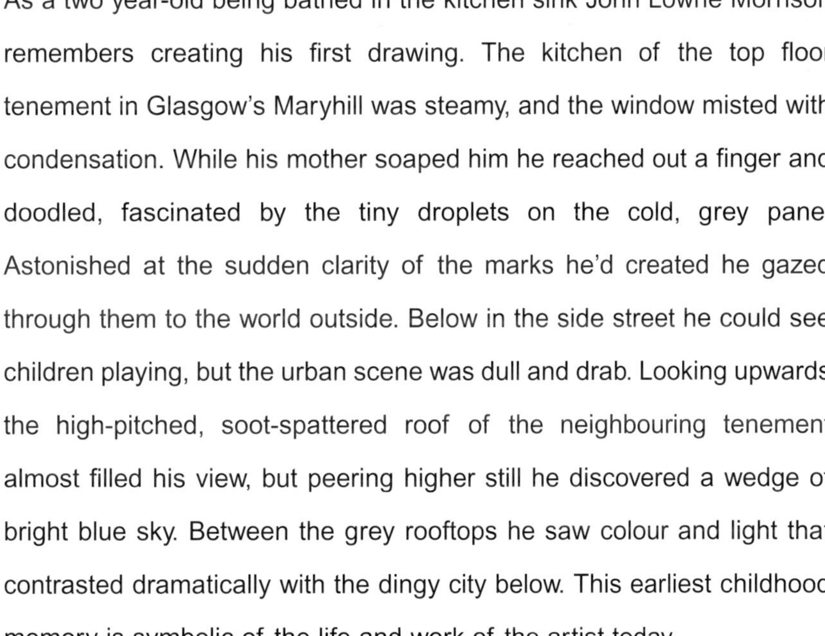

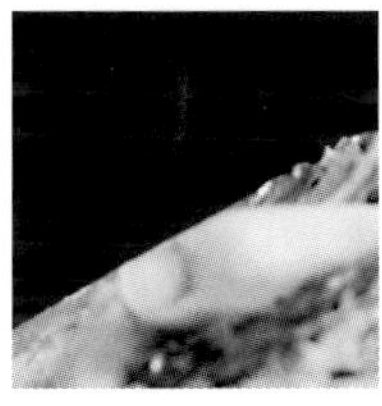

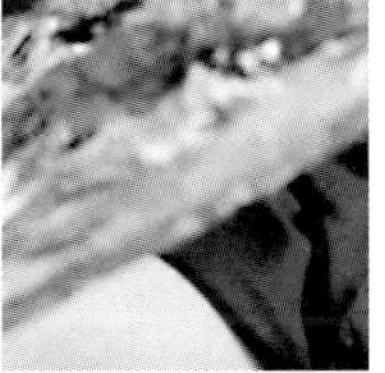

Born on the 15th December 1948, a second son to Murdo and Bessie Morrison (née Lowrie), John Lowrie Morrison lived at Queen's Cross, opposite Charles Rennie Mackintosh's church. John still recalls the beautiful church, as well as the huge marble fireplaces and bay windows of his first home. Whilst John was small the family moved to Glasgow's West End and here his mother, daughter of watercolour painter Henry Lowrie, gently nurtured the foundation of John's artistic career. Bessie Lowrie was gifted at drawing, secretly aspiring to teach art, but circumstances necessitated her leaving school at fourteen to work, and later on, as Bessie Morrison, motherhood pushed her ideals further away. Instead, she instilled her unfulfilled hopes and dreams into John. As a young man, Bessie's father had worked as a waiter in Montparnasse, that quarter of Paris alive with the colour and romance of the Impressionists who frequented it. Henry Lowrie's aspirations are unknown; although technically brilliant as a water-colourist he never made a living as an artist, becoming indentured to the Guild of Printers in London before moving to Glasgow and working as an insurance agent. His daughter's inherited artistic talent found an outlet making fancy chocolate boxes to supplement the family income. It was a job that Bessie kept all her working life, but as a young mother, she knew deep inside that her youngest son would one day be an artist. Perhaps it was because Lowrie artistic talents had been thwarted for two generations that Bessie was determined to develop in John a love of art from a very early age. Or did she have that intuitive inner knowledge that mothers sometimes possess?

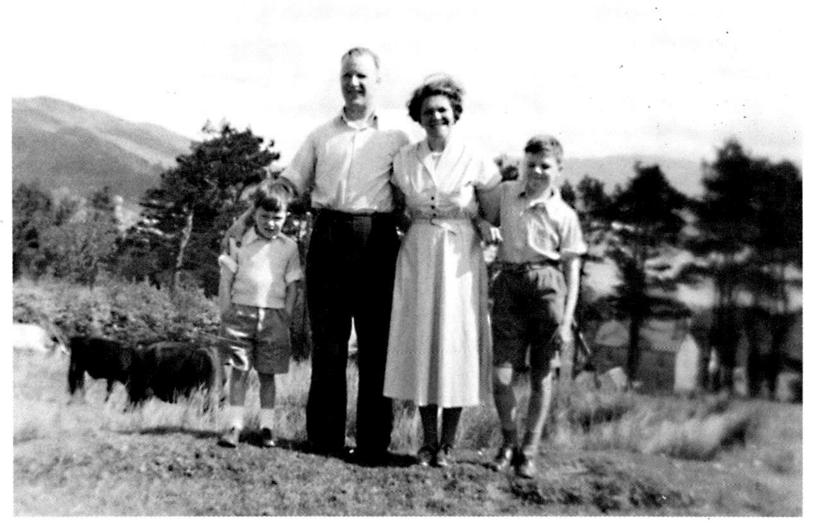

John and family, Tighnabruaich 1952

If Bessie was responsible for John's love of beauty in art (taking him to Kelvingrove Museum every Sunday after church in his pram, repeating 'Now you just sit there and look at that beautiful painting'), then his father Murdo (from the Isle of Harris) gave John a love of the countryside and especially the crofts. Bessie encouraged John to draw with the pastels she gave him when he was four, Murdo took the family on holidays 'doon the watter' to stay in 'wee but-n-bens' rented at Kames and Tighnabruaich. Murdo Morrison was a Postal and Telegraph Officer who worked hard to provide for his family. Despite living in a leafy suburb John loved the whole experience of getting away from the greys and browns of Glasgow's city streets, going through 'The Narrows' on the Waverley, or later driving by car to coastal villages with cottages just a step away from the waves. It was here that John developed his love of crofts, the sea, and the landscape of Argyll.

John was brought up to be God-fearing. He vividly remembers being seated by his mother in front of Salvador Dali's Christ and St John of the Cross (a painting of great beauty), going into Charles Rennie Mackintosh's church, and being frightened his first time at Sunday school by the Old Testament pictures of men with big beards! His early Christian upbringing developed in him a healthy respect for God that, in later life, formed the foundation of his respect for people.

Despite preferring (perhaps precociously) to experiment with the oil paints his mother had given him rather than play outside with other eight-year-olds, John was not a gentle retiring boy but one developing a quiet determination. He knew somehow that one day he would become a well known artist but he did not allow this inner feeling to let him rest on his laurels and he worked hard at school. As a pupil at Downhill Primary School he first experienced injustice when he was ridiculed by his teacher for saying, confidently, that he wanted to go to the Glasgow School of Art. The hoots of derision from teacher and friends angered young John and made him even more determined. His conviction wasn't diminished three years later when at Hyndland Secondary he was belted, six times, for asking as soon as he arrived 'when would he get art?' His anger at ridicule and his sense of injustice were character-forming childhood lessons that contributed to John's future success as a fair-minded teacher. As a youngster he was finding the strength not to have his aspirations demolished by taunts, or tawse. Deep inside the conviction was there - one day he *would* be a great artist.

Whilst Bessie's weekly visits to Kelvingrove Museum deepened John's love of art through talking about the paintings, two teachers at Downhill Primary made a positive contribution to his artistic education. The head teacher, Mr. Nicholson, realised the keen youngster's talent and actively promoted art, and his favourite teacher, Miss Don, made art part of the curriculum and not just something her pupils got on Friday afternoons if they'd been good. During John's last years at Downhill it was a fortnightly treat to visit the Kelvingrove Museum basements under the tutelage of the museum's education officer, Jean Irwin. Jean was a famous teacher who introduced John to geography, geology, anthropology and the history of the world. John thought it fantastic to be shown a film about the way the Inuit lived, then to be allowed to touch real 'Eskimo' clothes on life-size models and to inspect an authentic sealskin kayak. Jean Irwin succeeded in initiating a holistic view of life and the world in John and he loved these visits as much as the alternative - swimming in the local baths. It was, however, in the gruff, strict Mr Birnie at Hyndland Secondary that John found his first inspirational art teacher. John recalls being a 'wee bit frightened' of the man who kept his pupils on their toes in the first and second years. He soon realised as he progressed further up the school that there was nothing to be frightened of, as unlike some teachers who lost his respect because they assaulted pupils with the belt, the art teacher's 'bad temper' was just an act of defence disguising a very nice man. Mr Birnie taught John the rudiments of art design and the importance of drawing - skills often lacking in art students today. John was not alone in being inspired by Mr Birnie - in his year the record number of seven students went on to the Glasgow School of Art.

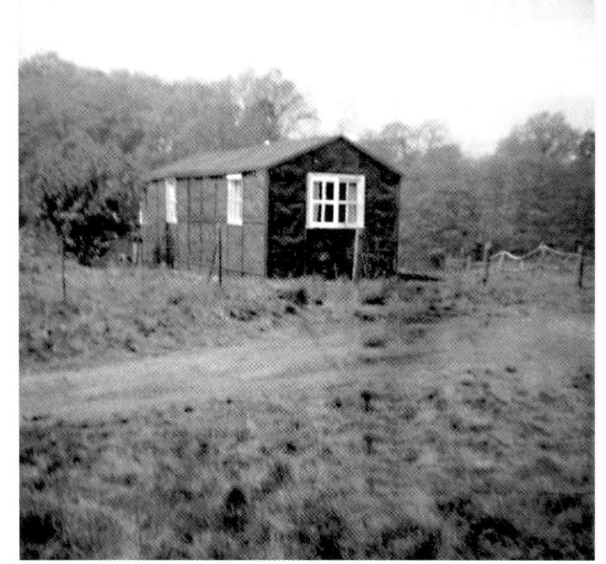

The "Hut" at Carbeth 1959

At seventeen years of age, John sold his first picture - his mother's cultural input and his good education 'paying off' earlier than expected! Displayed in a Glasgow Civic Art Exhibition at the McLellan Galleries, the painting sold for twenty-five pounds. In 1965 this was a small fortune to a teenager who was still two years away from his dream of attending Art College. John's school years had been dogged by bronchitis and pneumonia and he worked hard to make up ground lost through illness. While his school friends were kicking footballs around, John sat and painted. Family holidays were still spent in the countryside, his parents having acquired holiday 'huts' at Carbeth, ten miles north of Glasgow. Weekends were also spent there and it was around these green clapboard huts and in the surrounding hills that John confirmed his love of the countryside and found inspiration as an artist. The years moved on and while his friends were out discovering the distractions of girls, John's consuming passion was to stay in the family hut, summer and winter, without piped water or electricity, and to paint, and paint, and paint.

In 1967 John's childhood ambition came true and he enrolled as a student at the Glasgow School of Art, staying on until 1971. Content to soak up as much as possible, John wasn't a rebellious student. He felt that he had a great deal to learn and he realised that his tutors had a lot to give. Dan Ferguson particularly, (a 'smashing landscape painter') was a great mentor for this keen young student. Dan brought out the best in his scholars, treating them with respect and never putting them down. Even when students got things wrong Ferguson built them up and encouraged them, a sensitive way of teaching that John was to incorporate in his own particular teaching style in the future.

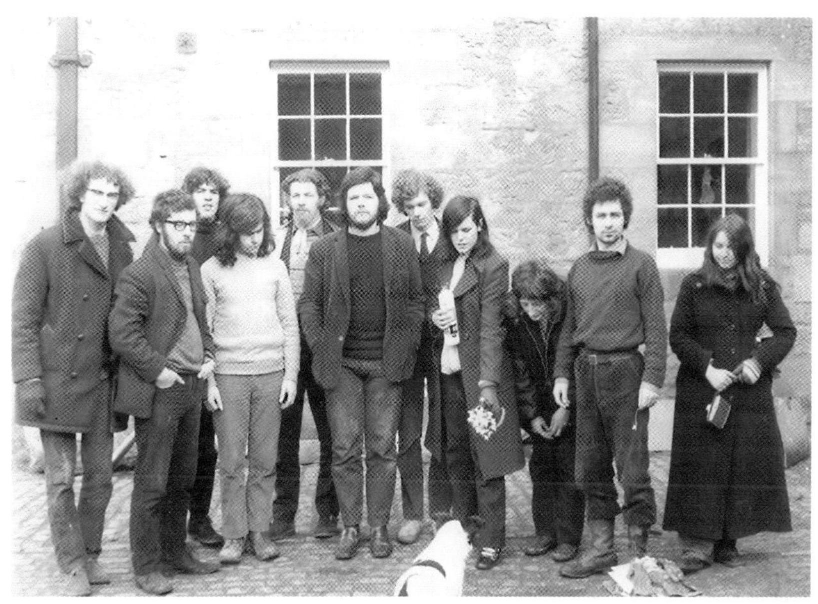

John (centre), Dan Ferguson (behind). GSA studio, Culzean Castle 1969

Meanwhile, Bessie and Murdo worked longer hours to help pay John's way through college. Bessie's place of work, Springer and Son, was near the art school and John would pop in to watch her at her bench deftly cutting pieces of strawboard to glue and stick, in a room with fifty other women. From seemingly nothing she created beautifully decorated tiered boxes. John treasures an oval shaped box with tiny fitted drawers decorated with tiny pearl handles that she made, and recalls that she always had 'a hint of glue' about her person. She had more than a hint of glue about her character, for Bessie stuck to her unstinting support and encouragement, backing John all the way.

1969 was a very important year in John's life, with make or break decisions. He had been enthralled by fashion and textiles both before going to art school and for his first two foundation years at college. John was so inspired by the head of the Textile Department, Bob Stewart, that he really thought he wanted to be a fashion designer. In his summer holidays John worked at Templeton's Carpets, designing circular Norsk rugs to sell to wealthy Arabs who insisted on buying 'the best carpets in the world'. John's work was downstairs in the design department but something must have led him upstairs - where he met his future wife Maureen, who was working in the shipping office. Returning to college John had to decide which path to pursue, Textile Design or Fine Art? He prayed for guidance as he walked towards the Fine Art building. Which should he choose? The question was agonising. A miasma of oil paint emanated from the Fine Art building and the smell locked into not only John's nose, but also his heart. It awakened some long buried dream in his soul. He was meant to be a painter and he 'followed the roar of the paint'.

At this time John sought peace in St Aloysius's Roman Catholic Church near the Art School. He had been introduced to this beautiful italianate church by his friend Michael Gilfedder and by Maureen, who was baptised a Roman Catholic. Instead of joining his contemporaries at college to relax over a cup of coffee John would often pop into the church to meditate. As a teenager he had drifted away from his religious upbringing but now the war in Vietnam and the arms build-up of two opposing super-powers gave John, by nature a questioning soul, much to contemplate. With so much fear and hatred in the world what was the meaning of life? He'd been brought up to love and respect God, but in the terrible conflict between people and nations, he now wondered - could God exist at all? Alone, in the quietness of the beautiful church, John was searching for an answer.

In December of 1969 (John was just twenty-one) he and Maureen attended a service at the Tron church in Glasgow. Three well-known celebrities were taking a special service on behalf of 'The Navigators' an organisation that distributed religious learning texts. They were Cliff Richard, James Fox, and Nigel Goodwin. The subject of the service was to do with the death of Christ and the meaning of life. Absorbed in the service, Christ's death was made so real to John by the words of Nigel Goodwin that the cloud of doubts, hopes, and questions with which he had struggled, suddenly cleared. By Maureen's side, John was suddenly convinced that to follow Christ was the way forward and that he wanted to be in God's hands for the rest of his life. A verse from psalm 23 repeated itself in his head 'And I shall dwell in the house of the Lord forever'.

John and Maureen visited Switzerland together in 1970 to stay at L'Abri Fellowship run by the Christian philosopher Dr Francis Schaeffer. It was here that John's artist's eyes opened on a brighter world. Clean air revealed the colours of the mountains and valleys in crystal clarity, the stark landscape looked clearer, more brilliant than he'd seen it before. Viewing creation from a high altitude can have a profound effect on people and John as an artist was deeply moved. Very early one morning John and Maureen climbed high in the mountains of the Dent de Midi near the Swiss border with Italy. Looking around they could see Italy to the south and Lake Geneva to the north. It was to prove a religious experience for them both. The awe-inspiring panorama of dazzling snow-covered peaks and deep shadowy valleys was cathartic. It hit them both, forcibly, that God was real - His character revealed through His creation. It was a 'born again' experience. Maureen made her own commitment as a Christian, deciding to become, like John, a member of the Church of Scotland and from that moment they moved ahead together. For his part, as an artist, John felt inspired to use a 'stronger palette', abandoning the safety of paler tones - not to paint lofty peaks, these huge edifices were beyond him then, but the high colours and what presaged them set his heart thumping! Another paving stone had been laid on the path before him.

In 1971 John won the W.O. Hutchinson drawing prize for outstanding achievement in drawing. The whole experience was wonderful for him. He had been engaged in post-graduate study at the Glasgow School of Art concentrating on figurative work, spending six months at a children's home working on his thesis (art therapy through the use of colour and gentle shapes

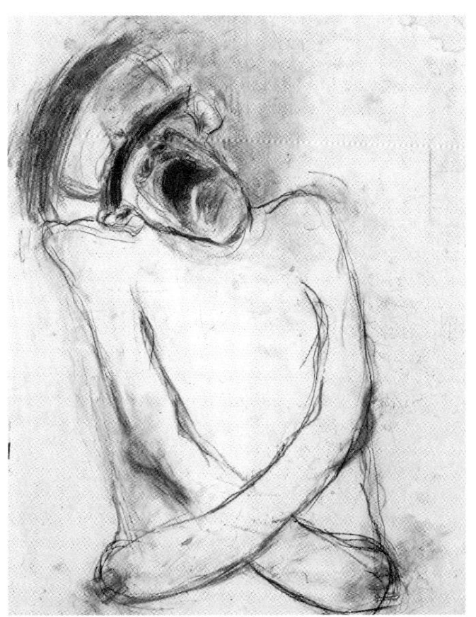

No Escape Except Through Christ 1971

'Enough' 1970

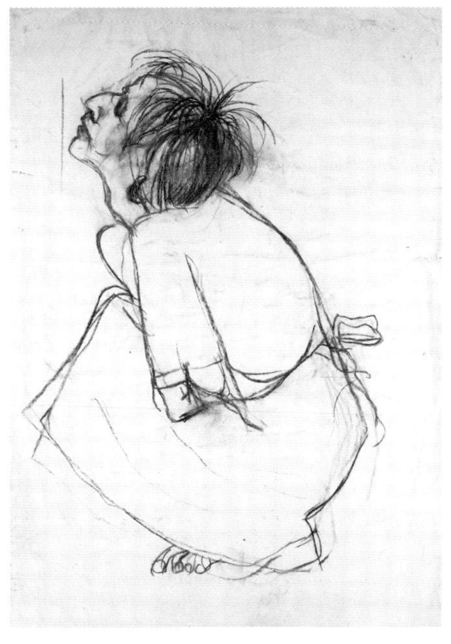

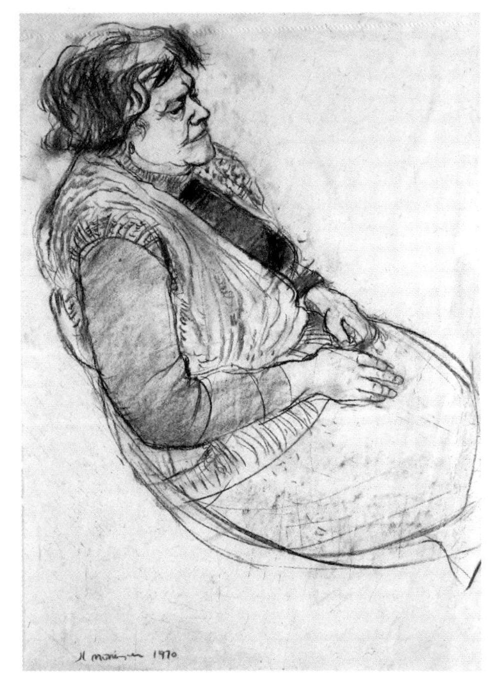

Artist's Mother 1970

Mo 1969

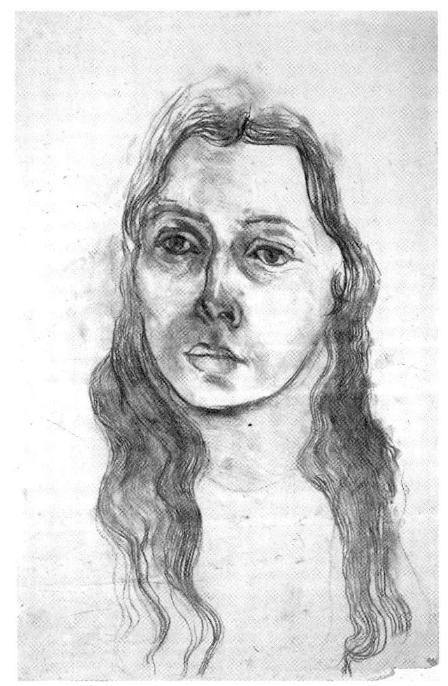

and forms). He also sketched patients at a hospital for the mentally ill, including a patient in a straightjacket and a distressed woman hunched in her white hospital robe rocking back and forth in a corner. The connection that John felt for them, apparent in his drawings, was a measure of his growing humanity and compassion. The W.O. Hutchinson award was for the best drawings of the year.

In 1972, aged twenty-four, John won a Landscape Scholarship from the Royal Academy Schools, London. The £300 prize was to give him the funds to travel. The other talented winners took themselves off to Italy or America, and John - well, he beat a track back to Carbeth. He created a studio out of one of the family huts and set out to paint the landscape around Campsie Fell. Despite having won a prestigious and lucrative award, and living in the place he deeply loved, John was not a happy artist. Seated at his easel he painstakingly, faithfully, recorded the hills with their volcanic outcrops but something was wrong. He was almost tearing his hair out with frustration - eventually all this pent up energy had to let rip. John jettisoned convention and the result was a wild, living, heaving landscape of bold strokes and pulsating colour. Like a stage in the metamorphosis of a caterpillar, John had shed his confining skin and emerged completely changed. Although he was not to use the distinctive signature for another decade or so, Jolomo's own inimitable, vibrant style of Expressionism had been born.

If a butterfly had been released then it was quickly captured and, apart from occasional flights of freedom, held prisoner for a while, for John was led towards teaching art as a career. One year spent at Jordanhill College in Glasgow saw him qualify with a Diploma in Education, and in 1973 he moved to Argyll to teach at Lochgilphead High School. Maureen and he were married and set up home in Ardrishaig. John continued to benefit from the love of the two most important women in his life. His mother was proud of his achievements and continued to encourage him, but it was Maureen, privy to his internalised self-doubt who constantly boosted his morale. Very, very good friends and confidants, side by side in bed at night she would quietly assure him that he would, one day, become a great artist. Although very grateful for his mother's encouragement, John maintains that Maureen was the person who helped him accept his identity as an artist, and that he might have given up his dream if it hadn't been for her faith and love. As he began his new career John discovered that he liked teaching, but from the word 'go' he simply couldn't commit himself heart and soul - he wanted to paint! Some force beyond his control perhaps had other plans…

Despite the vicissitudes of teaching John discovered that he was learning much from his pupils, including the adults who attended his art classes. At one stage he had many adults coming in and out of his lessons. Some were young, others aged seventy and over, and what they taught him was part of John's own ongoing experience of humanity, education and development of discipline. His skill in teaching meant that John also had success with students experiencing learning difficulties, put into his charge at school, more for occupational therapy than any hope of achievement. John thought differently, however, they challenged him and he challenged them back. He led them on by encouraging them. Inevitably teacher and pupils learnt from each other and some students achieved standard grades in art, even going on to pass further modules in photography.

The practice of teaching instilled a discipline into John that served him in good stead. Each day was run between six bells. John found himself on a treadmill. The bell rang, twenty pupils would arrive for an hour to do 'their thing', the bell would ring again, they departed and another twenty would arrive, and so on until the end of the day, five days a week, week in week out. During weekends he craved more free time for his own painting. When school vacation came around he felt like a wrung-out cloth - a feeling many teachers share! John gave out so much to his pupils that his own creative batteries needed time to recover their energy. On holidays at home or abroad with Maureen and later with their children in tow, he was impelled to visit museums, to stop wherever he saw an exciting composition, the need to recharge the artist in him driving him to photograph and sketch at every opportunity. His family was very patient with him, and it was Maureen, in need of rest from her own demanding career as a psychiatric nurse, who kicked a football around with their sons.

In 1978 John and Maureen moved to Tayvallich together with their young sons Calum and Peter. It must have felt like coming back home to the wee crofts that had so enthralled John as a lad on family holidays at Tighnabruaich. At their first home in Ardrishaig John had painted in a tiny studio he had made from a garden shed, selling his work to augment his small teacher's salary and to keep the bank manager at bay. At Tayvallich, where their third son Simon was born, he painted in the loft and continued to sell the occasional piece of work. In 1982 they visited his father's family croft at Kyles on Harris. This connection with his father's roots helped affirm his own love of those Hebridean cottages where the drama and pathos of history in other human lives had once played. He painted with a growing insight. In 1984 he visited Holland and found an affinity as he painted the old small homes of the Dutch peasants. In 1985 he began signing his paintings 'Jolomo'. It was a handle that had come to him in a moment of abstraction during a Latin lesson at school as he wrote the abbreviation of his names in his Latin book. Years later in college he learnt that the artist Oskar Kokoschka signed himself OK - a tongue in cheek signature that John thought quite

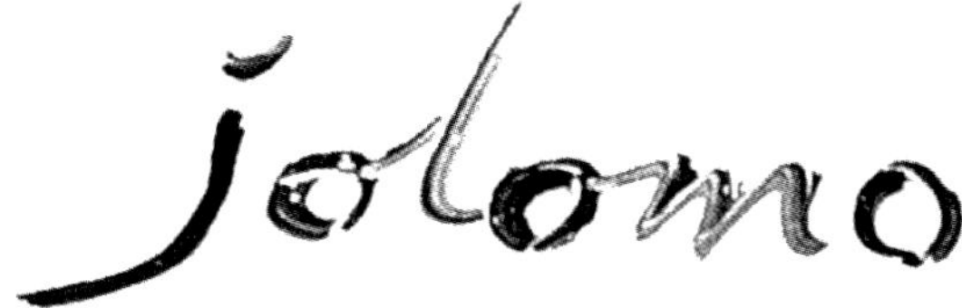

clever, so when he became bored with signing his work John Lowrie Morrison and wanted something shorter he recalled his old, self-given name Jolomo. Pronounced JoLOmo, (an unconscious emphasis on the Lowrie part of his name) it is John's trademark.

By 1988 fifteen years of teaching had accrued at Lochgilphead High School and John was promoted to Principal Teacher of Art - a position he held for six years. A fair-minded teacher who respected his students, John's teaching was both challenging and inspirational. Many of his pupils went on to study art in further education. These included his sons, Calum, Peter, and Simon, who have all inherited John's artistic talent. Calum (twenty-nine), studied Computer Graphics. He suffers from achondroplasia and spent many childhood years at the Princess Margaret Rose Hospital in Edinburgh, undergoing leg-lengthening operations that added five inches to his height.

His courage was acclaimed when he was one of just a handful of children who won the Children's Bravery Award. Calum now helps John with picture framing. Peter (twenty-seven) followed in his father's footsteps studying Fine Art at the Glasgow School of Art, and is now song-writer and lead guitarist with the successful Christian rock band 'Superhero'. Simon (twenty-one), a talented artist, is now John's 'right-hand man' with his own frame-making business providing his dad with many of his frames. John never expected or pressurised his sons to be artistic but perhaps it was inevitable that they should follow in his footsteps. John's maxim was (and still is) 'Everyone can create! You may not be a Rembrandt, or a great writer, or a sculptor but you can create. You are made in the image of God, and God created, therefore you can!'

From 1987 to 1988 John was stretched beyond his normal art teacher responsibilities. He was chosen to become the Technical and Vocational Educational Initiative Co-ordinator at Lochgilphead, a job that was akin to being assistant head. Although John knew very little about technology he was given the job of overseeing computers installed into each department because he was both diplomatic and assertive. Not everyone at Lochgilphead High School was equally keen to embrace new technology - especially those who couldn't cope with the weird new jargon, the computer language that John had to swallow, digest, and teach. John's persuasive powers (used on any Luddite sticking with the old ways) were employed less in the iron-fist-velvet-glove approach, rather in the more kindly 'I understand exactly how you feel, but let me show you the marvellous things that these new computers can do for your department...' He usually won the day.

In 1989 John was back painting in Holland, with a painting trip to the Loire following in 1990. Here he developed his use of high key colour. Another painting trip to South Uist in 1993 saw this develop further. It was around this time that John became a volunteer worker for the Gideons International, a group of professional people who provide Bibles not only to hotels and guest houses but to school children as well. He also became one of three Art Advisers for Strathclyde Region, a job that covered Argyll, Dumbarton and Glasgow North divisions. His educational work now took him from Cumbernauld to Tiree.

In 1995 John went to paint in the Duras region of southern France, reading and absorbing the geography and history of the area in order to understand its life. He picked up the vibes and translated them to his paintings, as he had with other places he'd painted. The sheer liberty of life in France, the sunshine and clement weather must have tugged at his artist's heartstrings. What was he doing still being a teacher? Surely the future held more challenges? Wasn't he meant to achieve more than this?

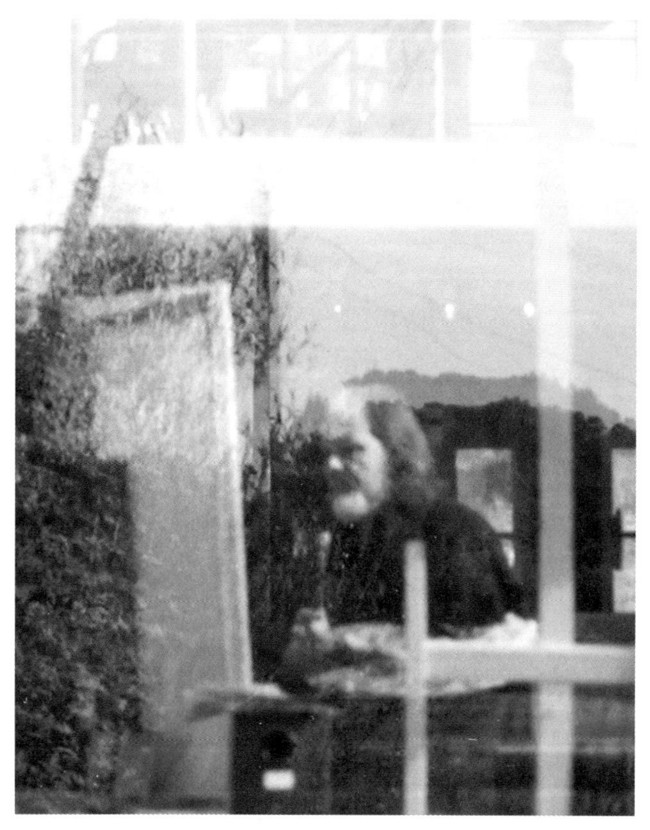

By 1997 John felt that after twenty-five years devoted to teaching he had really sacrificed enough to this field. It was time for him to move ahead in faith. He had come to the point when he felt God was saying to him 'get out'. When he broke the news to Maureen telling her that he felt God was telling him to give up his safe, salaried job she almost ran a mile! They prayed together with their friends David and Louise Logue and all of them felt that this was what John should do. God, however, had perhaps decided that this man of talent and energy could cope with another job as well. John may have been looking forward to the freedom of being a full-time artist but when he heard, after a church service, an inner voice say simply, 'John, you are going to be a *preacher* and a painter', he didn't run away, he knew God had spoken to him. He was willing to obey. There was, however, the little matter of earning a living and this relied, of course, upon him selling his work. His faith was tested at his first exhibition, a two-man show, where only two of his paintings sold. Three weeks later he had his second show. Would this go the same way? It was a nail-biting time but John's faith was rewarded with almost a sell-out. And so it has continued, year on year his sales increasing, with galleries throughout Britain clamouring for his work, so much so that John's phenomenal sales output today has reached the 'exponential'!

The years he dedicated to teaching now serve John well. A quarter of a century on the treadmill of a rigid timetable, rising early, juggling responsibilities, meeting targets and using different talents, are skills that enable John to cope with his present gargantuan workload as a committed painter and a committed preacher. An Elder in the Church of Scotland from the age of twenty-one, John's desire to offer himself for ministry was welcomed by South Argyll Presbytery. With their blessing, he enrolled on a Scottish Churches' Open College course to study to be a Reader (licensed to lead worship and preach within the Church of Scotland). For three years he became a distance-learning student, studying various modules and completing demanding essays in order to attain the Scottish Higher Diploma in Religious Studies accredited by Napier University. His teacher's ability to communicate assisted him in a calling he describes as a privilege: to lead people in worship. Writing the prayers and sermons for services occupy his evenings and may take all week to prepare but he does not necessarily feel he is there to put his own views. Just as he once taught, he tries to challenge people in his sermons, leading by encouragement, challenging in a gentle way. He gives his congregations something to think about in direct, simply-worded preaching that gets to the heart of the matter. John is rising to his calling, building confidence in what he feels he can say, respecting the congregations in the three churches of North Knapdale parish and gaining from their positive feedback. John lives by the message that he preaches: 'Life is about challenges - otherwise we don't move on'.

John now paints eight hours a day, six days a week, and preaches on many Sundays. He tours the islands of Mull, Iona, Ulva, Gigha, Islay, Luing and Seil, the Outer Hebrides, as well as Ardnamurchan, Kintyre and West Argyll, searching for scenes of beauty, colour and light. His paintings are snapped up from international exhibitions because of the feelings of joy and peace that they so vibrantly engender. He has painted in Normandy, exhibited in China and North America, and (closer to home 'though not on dry land') on the Caledonian-MacBrayne ferry: *M.V. Isle of Mull*. He has been commissioned by the Royal Navy to paint a picture of the *Ark Royal*, and he is the subject of a DVD film about his work, entitled 'I know where I'm going'. Life has become very successful but also very challenging and John proudly admits that he would not be where he is now without the help and support of his beloved Mo over the years. Maureen unselfishly gave up her job in psychiatric medicine to manage John's career. She now runs the administration side of the business - a huge amount of work - releasing John to concentrate on painting.

John's mother Bessie was very proud of his success, only revealing her secret yearning to have been an art teacher herself in a lucid moment during her last years when she was troubled by dementia. John, Maureen and their sons cared for her and sometimes she would slip quietly into John's studio to sit at his back and watch him work. In her later years Bessie may well have recalled their trips to see the paintings at Kelvingrove, the visits to churches, the holidays by the sea or in the country. Her son had achieved her ambition for him in more ways than one. Bessie Morrison died at Lochgilphead in June 2002. Just before she died John had been asked by Janet de Vigne of the Scottish Christian Press to paint the religious paintings that are now in this book. When Bessie watched him in his studio applying paint with palette knife and brush, intuitively marking the surface with his finger - would she have been taken back to the sink full of bubbles and her two year-old son doodling on the kitchen window? The light and the colour of that wedge of blue sky, discovered by serendipity that day when John looked up to heaven, have penetrated both his soul and the art that streams from it. High key colours are Jolomo's hallmark but it is the spirit of the man and his maker, distilled in them that makes every colourful painting such a joy to the eye.

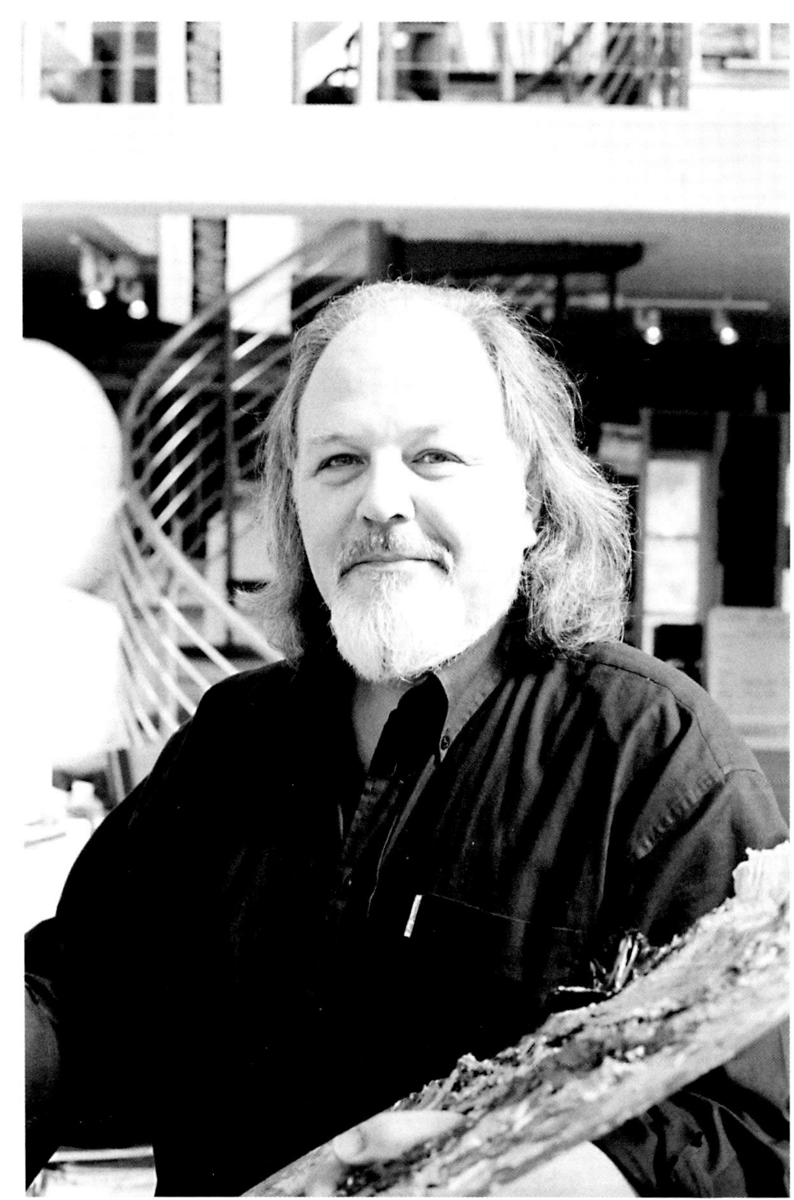

On Monday 2nd September 2002 John Lowrie Morrison was 'Set Apart' as a Reader in the Church of Scotland.

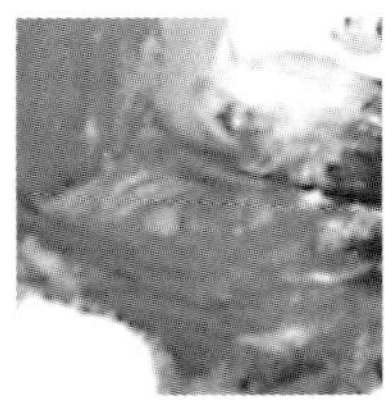

'I do not paint what I see but what affects me' is one of the fundamental statements about Expressionist painting. The Expressionist artist is said to endeavour to give 'external graphic form to internal anxiety'. The first of these statements holds true for all John Lowrie Morrison paintings, the second statement does not. In the case of expressionist paintings by Jolomo a unique definition is required. 'External graphic form to internal joy' perhaps, or 'colour, life, and spirit glorifying creation' better still. John's landscape expressionism is not angst-ridden. He does not have internal demons driving him to produce paintings akin to 'The Scream', but a deeply held love of his Maker and a desire to add beauty to the world.

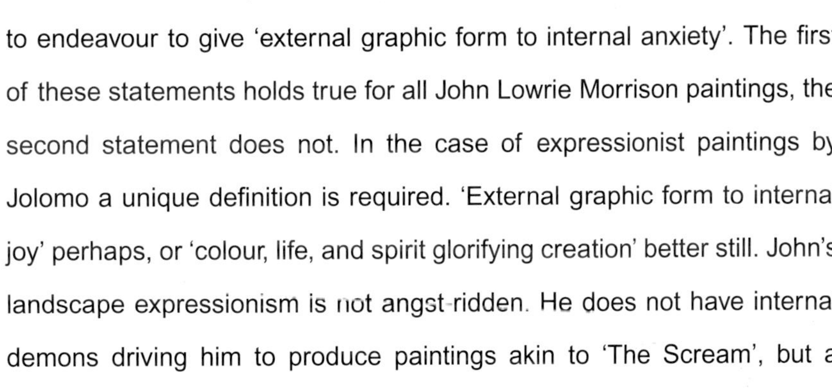

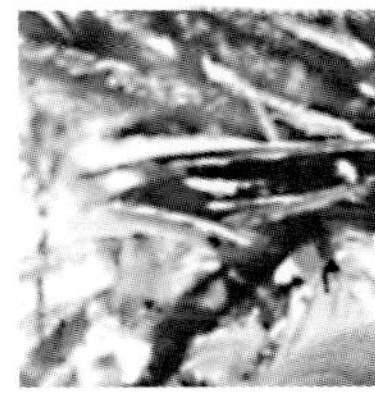

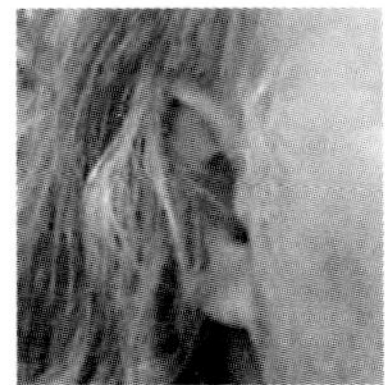

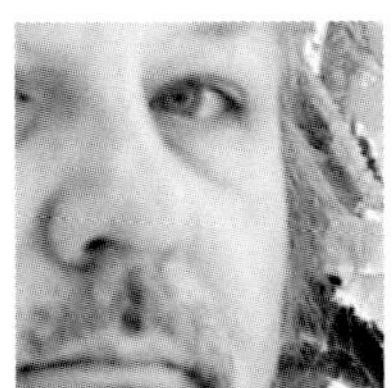

This book contains pictures dating from John's earliest days at the Glasgow School of Art, and the development of his unique style can be traced from his prize-winning figurative drawing through to the bold expressionistic strokes of his trademark oil painting today. This is the first time a retrospective of his work has been presented, and it is fascinating to watch John evolve into an expressionist. He admits that although he considers himself to be an expressionist artist, his paintings are not pure Expressionism. Pure expressionists stand at their easels not knowing how the end product will turn out; John often has a fair idea. Sometimes he says he will awaken with a picture vibrantly clear in his mind's eye and have to dash to his studio to paint what he's seen

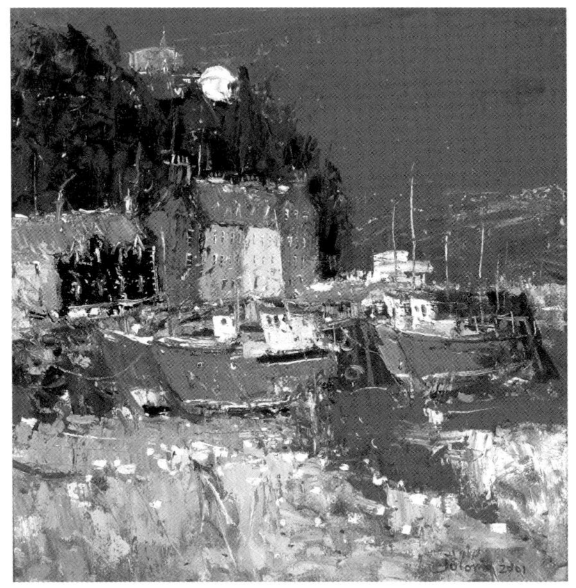

Moon Rise and Fishing Boats, Tobermory 2001

before the vision fades. He asserts his trust also in 'happy accidents', marks that arrive seemingly by themselves and that add to the picture. In the truest sense his paintings are not exactly what he sees, but they are what affects him, taking into account that a measure of Impressionism and a drop of the Scottish Colourists should be added. 'Jolomo Expressionism' is a hybrid of the best elements of the three.

Expressionists paint what *they* see. Coincidentally, SEE as a mnemonic epitomises the particular magic of a Jolomo landscape. S is for spirituality, E for exuberance, and E again for energy - three qualities synonymous with John himself. John sees, in the landscape and croft scenes that he paints, the lives of the people who lived there, the wind that blows around the chimney pots and corners of the houses, the intangible yet perceptible spirit of the place. By contrast his religious expressionist paintings capture the anguish inherent in the challenges and sacrifices of the subjects. Spirituality, exuberance, and energy are there too, although this time they come from even deeper within the man.

The hallmark of a Jolomo painting is the contrast in the light - John prefers 'The Dramatic'. The light of early morning and evening when the sun is low and contrasts are stronger gives the chiaroscuro effect that imparts a spiritual quality. Of the two, John prefers evenings. He is fascinated by night settings where moonrise and harvest moons add an ethereal quality to the composition. His enthusiasm for moonlit nights never ceases when each is so different. He finds moonlight stimulating because it subdues everything, even adding a touch of 'out of focus-ness' to the scene. He feels this quality enables viewers to 'escape' into his paintings if they feel the need.

The strength and vigour of each painting can be seen in the bold, broad strokes of oils spread by palette knife, brush, or finger. John achieves a balance between brush and knife as he sits at his easel rapidly covering the white board with saturated colour. He always works fast, (speed is part of John's persona), the white space quickly becomes awash with background tints, his precise brushwork deftly outlines the subject and landscape to come. Completely absorbed in his work, he is physically seated at his easel but spiritually, as through meditation, he says that he concentrates his awareness so that he is also far away feeling the breeze on his face, tasting the salt in the air, smelling the newly-scythed hay, hearing the flap of washing in the wind. The colours now focussed in his mind's eye are those same colours that he 'zoomed in on' when selecting the scene as a subject. He reduces greens, too dominant a hue, and sees the other colours of the landscape intensified. The vibrancy of these naturally subordinate colours, highlighting and contrasting in radiant high key tones, is part of the brilliance of John's Expressionism. Not only are his paintings alive, they pulsate with energy. His brush and knife strokes are intuitive; the painting takes on life and form because John is spiritually connected through it to the place it represents. A sketch or photo may be pinned to the edge of the easel, but he paints mainly from his mind's eye. When he perceives that light, colour, and form are balanced just right, he stops. John never 'over' paints - the results are startling in their simplicity. The effect is seismic.

Not every painting works. John starts each day with a period of quiet when he reads a portion of the Bible and then sets his work before God in prayer before he takes up the brush, asking that His spirit will work through it. He may complete a painting that is one of his best only to find that the next goes wrong or doesn't work because it is unbalanced. Balance is something that is central to his compositions - if it isn't there then the paint is scraped off and the offending image disappears. John will never let a painting get the better of him. Either it expresses what he sees or it is erased. Sometimes as many as one in four are rejected and each day it is a struggle to achieve his own standard of perfection. Anyone who imagines that Jolomo simply 'churns them out' should be a fly on the wall and watch.

This book represents a departure from Jolomo's norm in that the paintings he's best known for rarely contain figures. He feels that static figures can in some instances immobilise the picture, fixing it in space and time; while his croft scenes abound with as much life and activity as exists in the imagination of the viewer. You only have to stand and look to glimpse someone emerging from the door of a cottage (see *Croft by the Shore, Isle of Harris* 1998 page 51), or from behind

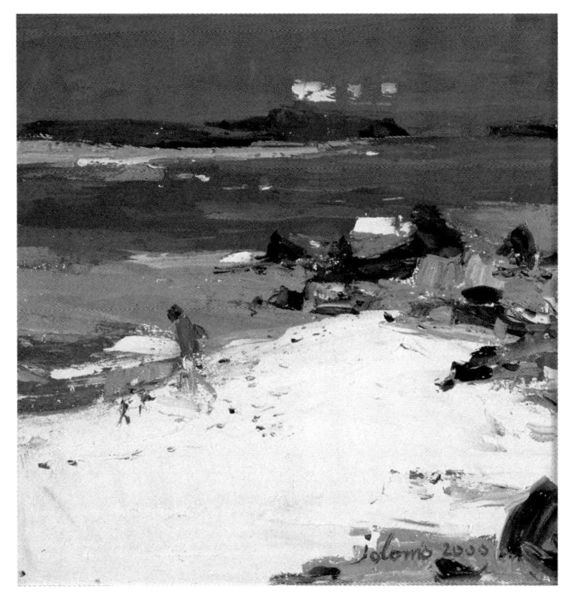
Mo & Corry, Iona 2000

a haystack (see *Haystacks, Iona* 1999 page 52), or around the corner of the house. Look for long enough and you might perceive the whole family. Look out to sea in any of John's beach scenes and you can visualise dolphins flying from the waves, an otter scrambling on to the rocks with a fish to eat, or the head of a seal emerging inquisitively to check you out. It's a very difficult thing to achieve but John really does capture the essence of the beings that live or lived there. However, remember also that this is the artist whose figurative work won him the W.O. Hutchinson drawing prize at Glasgow. The figures of *Mo and Corry*, (John's wife Maureen and spaniel Corryvreckan - page 53), in beach scenes on Iona, do not have an immobilising effect; on the contrary Mo's footsteps can be followed in the sand and this device gives the picture movement. You can go back over the painting almost frame by frame, even stopping the sequence to see that the blur near the tide-line is Corry digging a hole. But as a deliberate development for this project, John felt it was time for a new exploration of figurative work inspired by religious themes. Throughout his life as an artist, from student days onwards, he has continued to sketch biblical subjects (see *No escape - except through Christ* 1971, charcoal page 40, *Christ carrying the Cross* 1991, pen page 43); though he has never before painted them in oil. Seven paintings were created specifically for 'the Colour of Life', discussed later in the *Spirituality* section.

John has been quoted as saying 'In a sometimes depressing world, I want to create a feeling of joy and happiness, with high key colour and vibrant style'. The men and women of the Royal Navy aboard the *Ark Royal* could attest to his success - many spend each week of duty with little time away from the ship - grey decks, grey walls. A dozen Jolomo prints form the 'windows' of this unnatural world, hanging in ward and mess rooms, helping to counter the stress of living in a landscape of riveted steel. The pictures are definitely therapeutic. On learning that they had bought so many prints, John presented the *Ark Royal's* company with a painting of Tobermory, where thousands of naval conscripts had trained in WWII. A typically generous gesture - the famously vibrant colours of Mull's burgh must surely lift the company's spirits.

Colour therapy has an undoubted healing effect. Colour has a profound effect on us at all levels, physical, mental, and emotional. Colour dominates our lives and affects our moods. At one end of the spectrum, red is exciting, orange is warm and energising, whilst yellow stimulates mental activity and promotes a feeling of confidence. In the middle, green balances and harmonises. At the other end blue, the colour of communication, is calming and healing, indigo helps intuition, whilst violet heightens awareness. White contains all colours, emphasises purity, illuminates thoughts and gives clarity. Black used with another colour enhances the energy of that second colour and stimulates inner reflection. Colour is energy. It is light of varying wavelengths. Light influences the activity of the pineal gland, which regulates the release of neurotransmitters (message senders within the brain) and the functioning of some hormones. Scientific studies have proved that different colours have effects on emotions and behaviour. So if colour is a *way* of life, what then is 'the Colour of Life'?

Happiness and positive feelings are emotions stirred by Jolomo landscapes. John believes in colour therapy and has both consciously and unconsciously used therapeutic colours in his pictures. His use of colour is intuitive and he believes it is not the brightness as such but the combination of and the use of colours, the texture and balance, which is healing. He will consciously balance complimentary or contrasting colour, and he even uses a strong colour such as red or bright green to buttress a falling down pole, house or chimney. John says he has sometimes wondered whether he actually sees colours brighter than most people do. If he sees something colourful within a landscape, he 'zooms in', seeing only that. On a walk along a rocky shore on a grey day his eyes will focus on a patch of bright orange lichen, or glistening seaweed. The clouds may part and suddenly there's an iridescent light, say sunbeams illuminating a field of corn stubble. When John sees the colour he multiplies the effect, going for the beauty.

Green is not a colour that John uses much. He regards green as an easy colour, a colour that people expect. Landscapes are green and people expect them to be painted green. It's that expectation that makes John use the colour sparingly, although he has now concocted his own shade of emerald green that is sufficiently vibrant and strong for him to want to use more. It has more depth - is more … other-worldly, somehow. Blue on the other hand he uses lavishly. Blue has a purity that 'zings' out at him. Other colours may seem just as bright, but for John the depths of blue tones have a spirituality and purity that speak to him. It is also an 'awakening' colour in John's paintings. He believes that blue can go either way: 'blue borders on the dark side of ourselves, but also on the lighter side'. A painting in different shades of blue has a romantic sense of the past. John also feels it also has a calming, healing effect. It is not, however, the colour itself, but the balance of blue with high key colours of reds, yellows, and greens that give the viewer of John's dominantly cobalt or cerulean paintings a sense of happiness. John thinks that almost totally blue pictures have an aura of unhappiness about them if they have no bright yellow to balance the colour. He's not happy with them if they lack contrast to lift them and yet his blue paintings sell well. Clearly the blue has a positive effect on people's psyche and possibly a healing vibration. Painting is a therapeutic activity for John himself, which leads to an intriguing question - where does John find all his energy? He admits to being full of 'total energy' all the time and says he doesn't know where it comes from.

'Beauty has a healing power' is a saying of Monet's often quoted by John. Certainly Monet's colourful canvases affect viewers positively, but their delicate pastel shades are quite different from the kaleidoscope of saturated colour that comprises a Jolomo. Monet's paintings of his garden at Giverney induce a dream-like state of relaxation, Jolomo's by contrast stimulate. This is how John wants them to be because, he maintains, 'life is not easy'. John admits to being in another world when he's painting. He's so totally focused that someone can speak to him and he doesn't hear them. He feels he has to 'go away' in order to create properly. Is it this otherworldliness translated into his paintings that makes them uplifting? Certainly owners of his paintings find, when they are feeling jaded, that a look at their Jolomo raises their spirits and re-energises them.

Most people would acknowledge that creativity of any kind is an energy consuming process. Creative people are exhausted after producing their handiwork, especially if it involves mental and physical activity, more so if it's a relentless eight hours, six days a week. John averages four paintings a day, nearly one hundred a month, and over a thousand paintings a year (allowing for holidays) if he is on target. It is an incredible output. How does he do it? Perhaps the answer lies in the 'perpetual energy' cycle that is unique to John. Could it be that his boundless drive is the result of massive, continual, self-administered doses of colour therapy, coupled with an ongoing, energising positive feedback from his own landscapes? John, surprised by the strength of intensity that grips him when he is painting, admits that he gets depressed when he stops. Additional energy is certainly

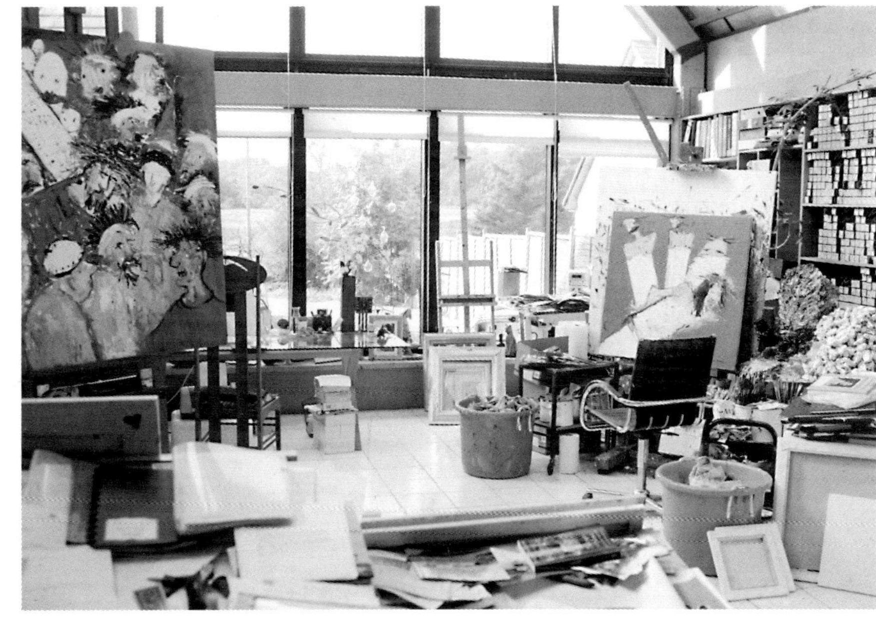

generated by use of high key colours, and he knows that to an extent the satisfaction gained from each newly completed picture gives him his unique get-up-and-go. But surely personal satisfaction and vibrant colour alone are not the answer to John's 'perpetual energy cycle'. Everyone knows that energy originates from the sun. Perhaps proximity to light, reflecting and reproducing its effects energises John?

The working title of *The Colour of Life* was 'Challenges and Sacrifices' - the subject of John's religious paintings. Do challenges and sacrifices make a difference to the *colour* of our lives? Without them would we miss out on the vibrant colours of life? Without the contrast of light and dark experiences, life would be dull and flat. By living up to challenges, by accepting sacrifices, do we colour the colourless by living life to the full, rather than by half-measures? The spectrum we recognise in our world comes from the light energy of solar rays selectively absorbed and reflected. But the *colour* in our lives, many would say, comes from a universal light, a divinity that is the 'Light of the World'. This pure light is also selectively absorbed and reflected, but produces the bright and clear spiritual colours that bring about joy, happiness, peace, enchantment, and wonder.

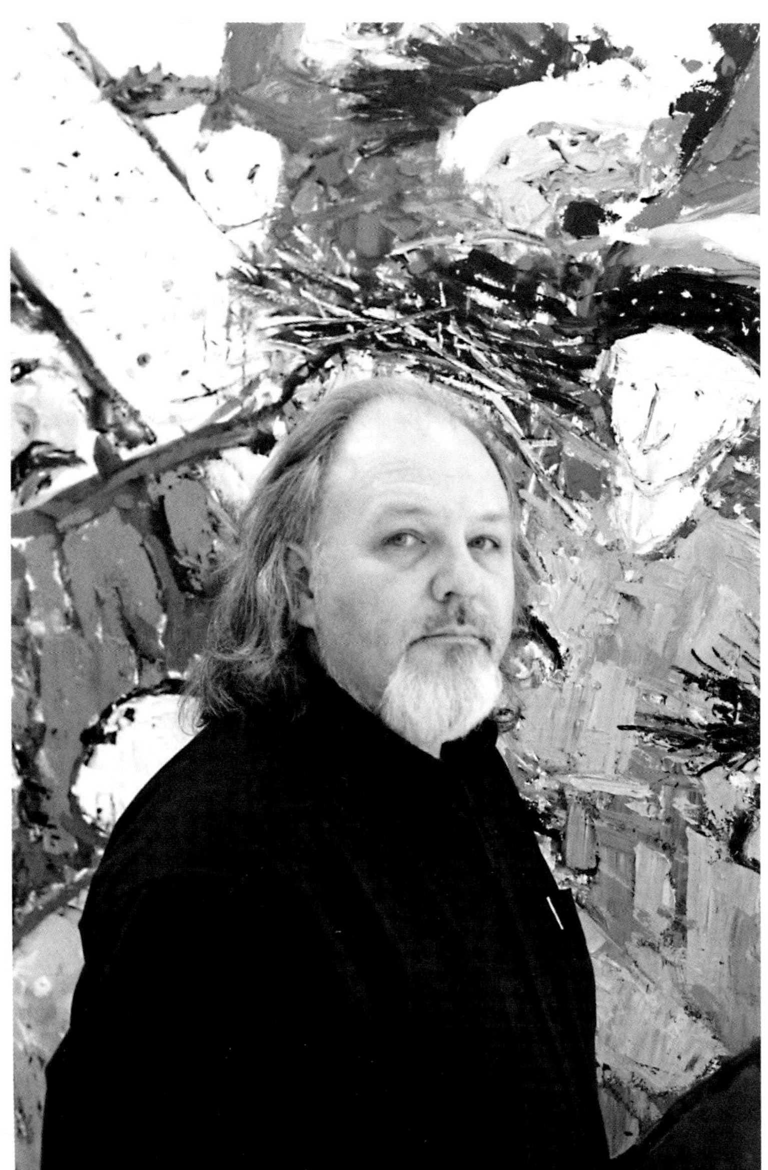

When John takes a pure white canvas and applies the colours that energise him, perhaps he is acting somehow as a prism; his unique expressionism can be seen not merely as solar but universal. In painting not so much what he sees as what affects him, is the man John Lowrie Morrison, an active Christian, a link with that light that is 'The Colour of Life'? Is that 'perpetual energy', a universal, spiritual energy? The 'colours of life' are white light, split into many colours; working through John's 'prismatic interface', which is translated into his paintings - is the Colour of Life - love?

spirituality in art

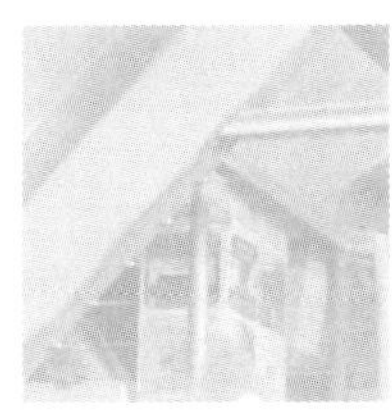

If the Colour of Life is Love, and God is Love, then it is John's human response to God in love that has led him to paint these expressionist religious works. Expressionists paint what they *feel*; and John's innermost feelings take form on canvas in the creation of these seven paintings of Biblical stories, one from the Old Testament and six from the New Testament. To paint what you *feel,* you have to *see* in your mind's eye with a compelling emotional honesty. 'Seeing' can be superficial and light-hearted if you want it to be, or it can penetrate far deeper. To paint religious scenes that convey real meaning the Expressionist has to draw from the deep heart - the very foundation of his human experience. He has to become a witness to be awed, amazed, terrified, or desolated, an invisible bystander at the event, transported back through layers of time and experience. What John *saw* in his mind's eye, and what he felt as a Christian as he painted these biblically-inspired images, had the opposite effect on him from his energy-giving landscape paintings. Both are richly spiritual, but instead of the *vibrancy* and *exuberance* of his landscapes, the religious works here, created for *The Colour of Life,* are epitomised by *angst* offset by sheer *wonder*. John feels that his experience in painting these is a measure of his love for God - both wonderful and awful, a 'see-saw' of emotions where he felt both drained and energised - and the experience which he distilled into the paintings.

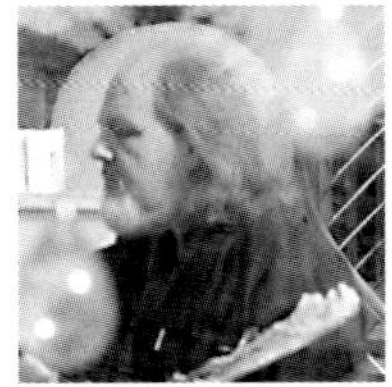

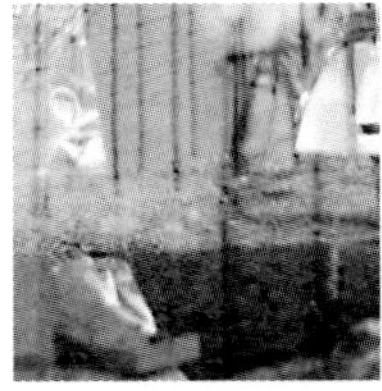

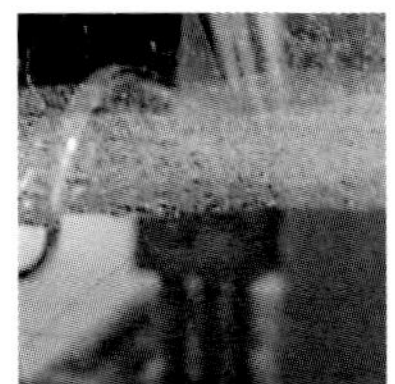

In December 2000 John was quoted as saying that he had no intention of producing religious paintings; so what made him change his mind? John says simply and emphatically that it was God. Although throughout his life as an artist, from his student days until today, he has drawn hundreds of sketches from religious themes he did not feel up till the present that he had the ability to produce any major painting. (See *No Escape - except through Christ* 1971 page 40). The idea that he might like to try came to him six months before this book was commissioned. To produce the seven new works featured here has been a challenge, but a challenge in which he has been helped. John always sets his daily work before God and these paintings, slowly and thoughtfully constructed over many days, called for more prayer than usual. Some paintings were envisioned, others drawn from the deep heart - the true expressionism that springs from the soul. John believes that these religious paintings are no more *spiritual* than his landscapes. He is emphatic that a painting does not have to have a religious theme to be spiritual, for when painting a landscape it is the spirit of the subject that he is trying to get across. He succeeds in the open communication of his own love of God, but there are many other levels of his art that will speak uniquely to every viewer. His earlier work, particularly the drawings of the hungry or the sick (see *Biafra* 1970 - *Malawi* 2002 page 37 and *Dementia* 1972, page 34) show the compassion he feels for humanity, a love fuelled by Christ's love for him.

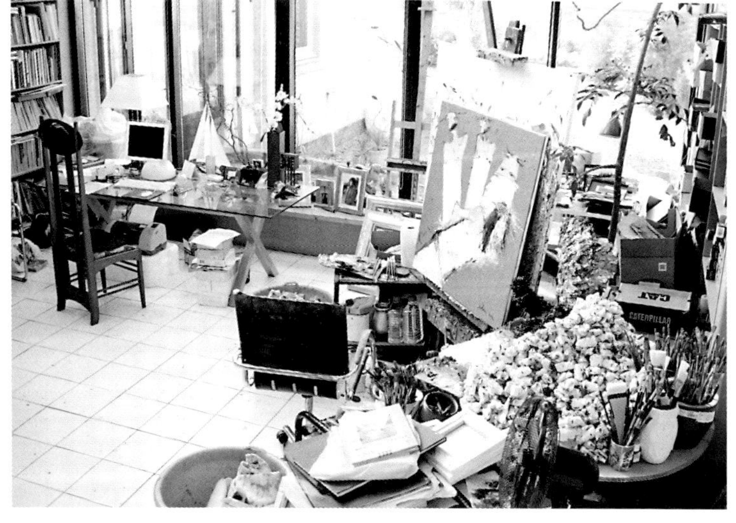

John paints in a huge, light, airy studio connected to his home where family members are free to come and go as they please. Sometimes they are ignored when John is 'far away', holding in his mind some beautiful Argyll landscape while transferring it to the canvas. Often they join him for a coffee and a chat, but when engaged on the religious works for the book, John found he could not stand to be interrupted at all. He found people a distraction and simply had to be on his own, without possibility of disturbance even from the 'phone. He had to become so totally focussed in order to bring out his feelings that any little thing, a fly buzzing or even the sun, became an annoyance.

Overcoming diversions, he could eventually become really connected to the 'deep heart'.

The Ram in the Thicket (page 63) was John's first painting for *The Colour of Life,* and is represented on the front cover. The idea for the composition, John says, had been growing inside him over the past twenty years. John's inspiration was Abraham's total faith and submission to God, in that he was prepared to sacrifice the thing he loved most - his son Isaac. Frightened and intrigued by the story at Sunday school, young John had found the awful command difficult to associate with a God of love. With the wisdom and understanding that comes with age, John now believes that we are all called upon to make sacrifices in our lives; our challenge is to rise to that sacrifice, however difficult it may be. Abraham's obedience to God was tested but his hand was to be divinely stayed before slaying his son (a right of paterfamilias in 2000 BC). The moon above Abraham's head is significant - besides representing the god Sin (the religion of Ur that Abraham forsook to follow the one true God) the full moon is a particular love of John's because it lightens the darkness of night. In this case the moon symbolises the light in the darkness by which God has shown Abraham the light of sacrifice.

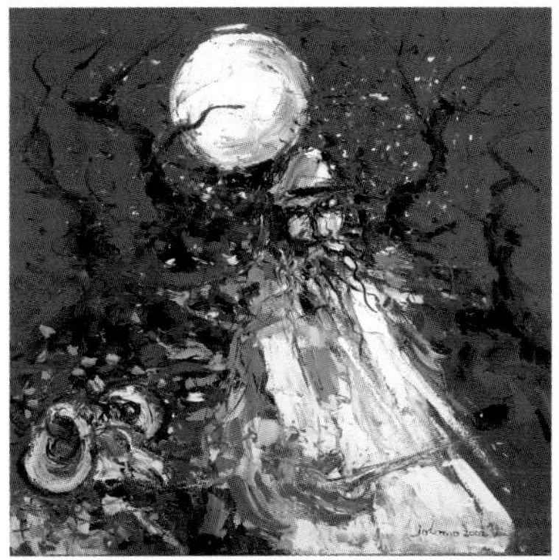

The Ram in the Thicket 2002

Unlike many painters of religious works John does not go for comfortable images or cosy biblical themes; he challenges his viewers to confront uncomfortable images that are expressive. In **Christ challenges the demons** (page 65) movement in the picture is dynamic. Christ's hand is featured, powerfully yet gently rebuking the demon - cosmically dissipating the powerful but weaker force of evil. John uses a touch of Fauvism here, painting the malevolent spirit emerald green to depict malice and wickedness, whilst Christ's head is covered in reverence to God through whom he receives his power. The limbless demon has a feeling of bondage about him even as he dissolves into the blue background.

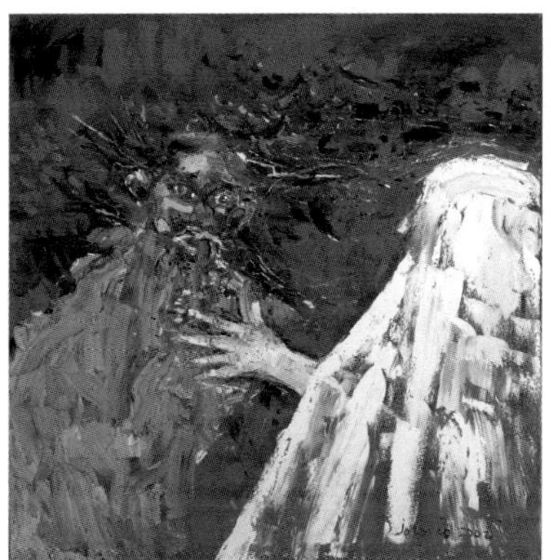

Christ challenges the Demon 2002

Lazarus, come out! (page 67): Although also featuring the hand of Christ and a cosmic force, this painting is by comparison joyful rather than forbidding. A cadaver of four days, bandaged from head to foot and laid in the grave, Lazarus is commanded by Jesus in the words of the title and the miracle of resurrection happens. One can feel as well as see the energy released as the strips

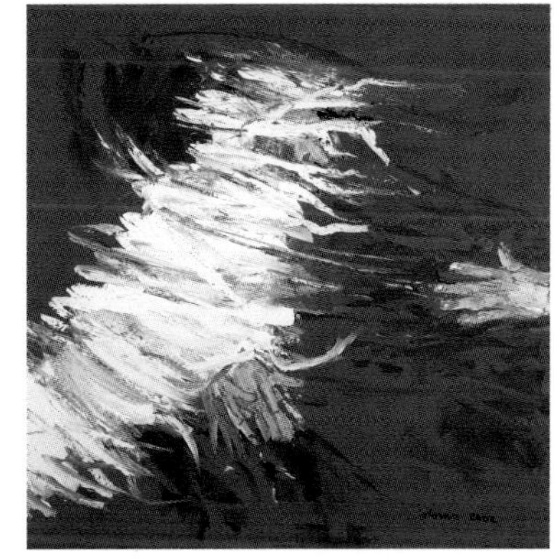

Lazarus, come out! 2002

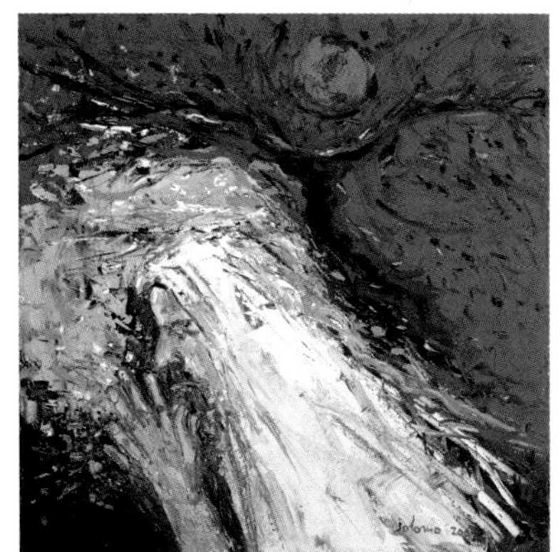

Shadow of the Cross 2002

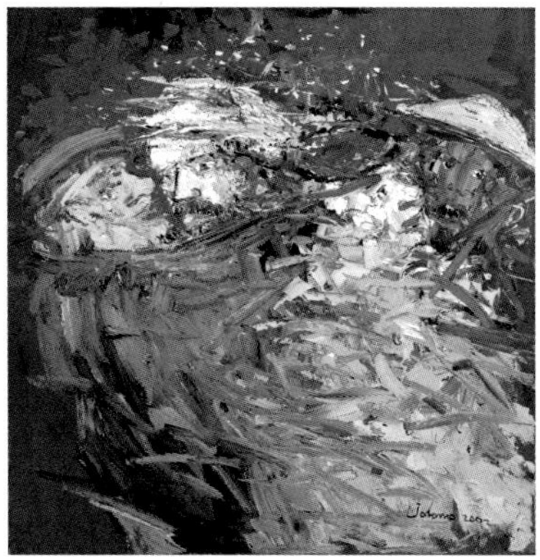

The Judas Kiss 2002

of linen burst and Lazarus' hands reach out to greet his Lord, his face marginally behind in the race to break free. Brush-strokes of white, against the blues, show the spiritual movement in the scene. This sense of movement draws the eye to Jesus' hand, where discrete red marks emanate from the fingertips. Thin traces of red paint signify John's belief that God is more powerful than death, the sparks recharging dead Lazarus, challenging death to 'get lost' as the mortal is reprieved.

While Christ could oppose death (challenging and defeating it in the case of Lazarus) the knowledge of His own approaching death still presented an agonising choice. The painting **Shadow of the Cross** (page 69) depicts that agony: the short-term, easy option of continuing to live with his mission unfulfilled, versus the consequence of obedience - a hideous, terrible death from which a lasting victory for humanity would arise. Here we see the face of Jesus (from the side) properly for the first time - it is a strong face, yet displaying the frailty and pain of a human. Christ's hands feature again, gripped in anguish but strong in supplication, wanting 'the cup to pass from him' but knowing that it should not. The shadow of the tree of crucifixion looms above his head surmounted by a blood-red moon, symbolism that John uses to express Christ's dilemma. The night sky is dark, yet there is spiritual activity in the private conversation going on between Father and Son. An aura of orange with red marks surrounds Jesus' covered head and hands. The aura is not a halo as such but John's way of showing the intense spiritual energy emanating from Christ, the warmth of His love and obedience as He accepts the challenge of His own bodily sacrifice. The painting is divided diagonally from top left to bottom right. The use of a white Jewish head-dress should impart a feeling of peace in the painting's lower half, but the tree, the ominous aggressive moon, and the marks of 'spiritual activity' in the top triangle create a terrible tension. The conflict is tangible, the outcome still in the balance.

The stillness of Christ deep in prayer contrasts dramatically with the frenzied activity of **The Judas Kiss** (page 71). The four figures, Judas, Jesus, Peter, and the servant Malchus, have been in John's mind and on his sketchpad over and over again, for 30 years. There is so much going on in this busy picture that one needs to look from left to right at each figure in turn, take in the action, and then go back to review it all once more. In this painting John has shown Christ's face more fully than in any other. The face is strong with a hint of anger and a suggestion of submission. The tiredness and the strain of His prayers, alone at Gethsemane, show in the pallor of His face. The marks about His head show the spiritual interplay, perhaps His sorrow, and even compassion for the approaching sinner, as treacherous Judas identifies Jesus with his kiss. The greed and sinfulness of Judas is symbolised by a yellow, hideous face, and green shapeless body that seems, at that moment, to encircle Jesus. Peter meanwhile is caught up in vigorous defence, slicing the ear from the intruding, surprised servant Malchus. Peter is unaware in the heat of the moment that his master has been betrayed. John had attempted many times over the years to paint a face of Christ, admitting it is 'an impossibly difficult task to paint God in the form of a man'. In *The Judas Kiss* he has consciously tried to create a strong face whose lines express anger, fear, compassion, sorrow, and pain. If you look you can see all these emotions played out in that drained expression as the action continues; John has achieved a whole movie in a single frame.

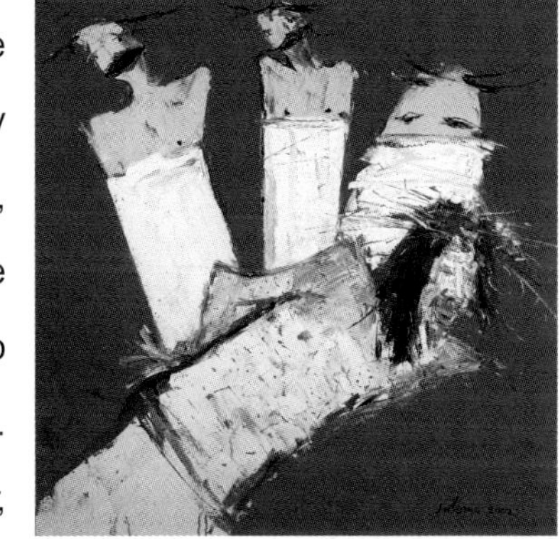

Christ Mocked 2002

John was very focussed for his painting of **Christ Mocked** (page 73) and the painting took form very quickly. Having been told of the devastating construction of a 'cat o' nine tails' - with which Jesus was flogged - John must have endured his own pain at the thought of such gratuitous torture as he brushed red, painted 'lacerations' across the vulnerable white flesh of the bent, bound body. Christ's face here is a tragic mask of suffering. Haggard, his aura is reduced to a few dying sparks. By contrast, the spirits of evil are in the ascendant, personified in the guards. John feels that this was probably Christ's lowest point before his crucifixion and he has expressed the tension between good and evil by using distortion, Christ leaning one way whilst the jubilant demons rise up in the air over him. For John the shapeless, hideous creatures in their straitjackets personify the pernicious evil of all torturers.

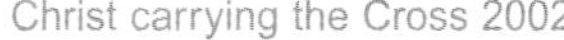

Christ carrying the Cross 2002

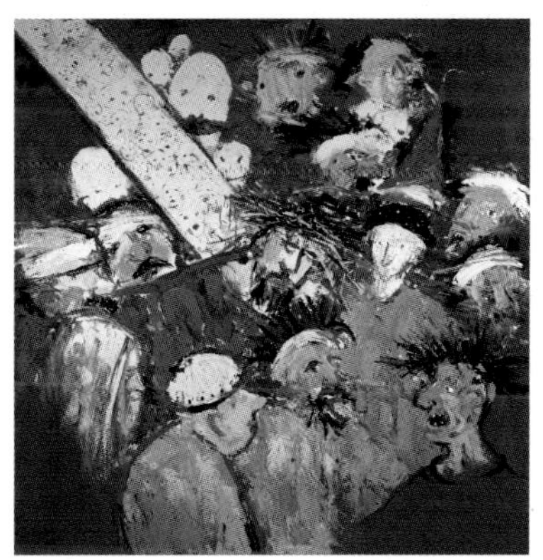

Christ carrying the Cross (page 75) is John's largest religious painting - 'the big one'. It is not meant to be a literal depiction of Christ carrying the cross along the Via Dolorosa surrounded by crowds lining the route; rather it shows images of things going on round about him. Graphic rather than literal, the simple and submissive figure of Christ, eyes downcast, is encircled by faces and figures, each with its own story in John's picture of this awful procession. Christ himself is physically bent under the weight of the cross; representing the sins of the world depicted in the palimpsest faces of murdered children. Close up against Jesus is a wizard. His enemy, the 'greatest magician' in the land - and he has come to see Him die! You can see the delight on the smug face, the gleeful beady eyes feeding on Christ's misfortune. You can almost hear the evil chuckle of 'get yourself out of this, if you're *really* so clever,' and the hiss of 'I'm a better magician than you!' Again, the green colour portraying evil partly encompasses Christ, whilst the pointed chin, nose and hat of the wizard rise above His head triumphantly. John has always had a clear mental picture of this character and so he says that this part of the painting came together quite quickly. The characters with 'bandages' around their heads represent soldiers, including the figure naked to the waist, and the figure at the front wearing a helmet. John envisaged them on the hot Friday night having to march out of Jerusalem up a dusty hillside to toil and sweat erecting a cross, the 'crucifixion detail' - jeering as they take this 'felon' to be punished. For the most part their attitude is 'rather him than me!' - no more emotion than that, yet John has painted one who is perturbed. You can see his face looking over Christ's shoulder, his eyes questioning. He's sympathetic, he isn't sure. Those who are sure are the sad-faced figures behind the wizard. Their world is collapsing around them, you can feel their hopelessness as their hoped-for king drags himself past, staggering further along the road to Calvary. At bottom right a Pharisee hurls insults at the 'blasphemer', his sardonic grimace contorting a sanctimonious face. At the top left, five demonic faces gloat over the tragic scene. Closest to Jesus, and yet alone in her grief, is his mother Mary, her face blue-white and drained of blood. Powerless to help, she watches him as he is led away to be murdered. John has painted her wistful face with such compassion, it is as though her own life is being sucked out and she is dying with her beloved son. John's ability to detail such suffering in this tragic procession gives the viewer a window into the intensity of the Via Dolorosa. He did not, could not, paint this in one session; it took him a long time and it consumed his own vitality.

These are the first Jolomo religious paintings but they will not be the last. John says he feels a great deal more inside him yet to come out and he's grateful to be free of financial constraints so that he can paint more biblical scenes. Now he has arrived at a depth of Christian understanding that has enabled him to produce this expressive work - he feels almost as though a raw nerve has been exposed. In the future he wants to explore his Christian feelings more, knowing that as his understanding increases, his artistic work can only get better.

John was deeply challenged by these seven paintings. 'I do not paint what I *see*, but what affects me' - the fundamental statement of Expressionism - can be expressed in John's case as 'I painted what I *saw* deep within my mind's eye, in a graphic form showing how my subjects affected me'. John sacrificed an incalculable amount of emotional energy as he painted what he saw, the spirituality, the angst, and the wonder of these Bible stories. His energy is instilled and encapsulated forever in each painting and now anyone can tap into those spiritual reserves. His personal 'see-saw' of energy, increased when painting vibrant landscapes, and depleted in painting religious scenes, remains a mystery. In his landscape painting, 'the Colour of Life' is Love, and if God *is* Love, and if these paintings *give* John energy, then in his religious painting is not also 'the Colour of Life' the love that John has *given back* to God by rising to life's challenges and accepting life's sacrifices?

John Lowrie Morrison is an expressionist artist of rare spiritual sensitivity whose paintings communicate directly with the hearts and often with the souls of his viewers. His love for humanity is apparent, his love for God undoubted.

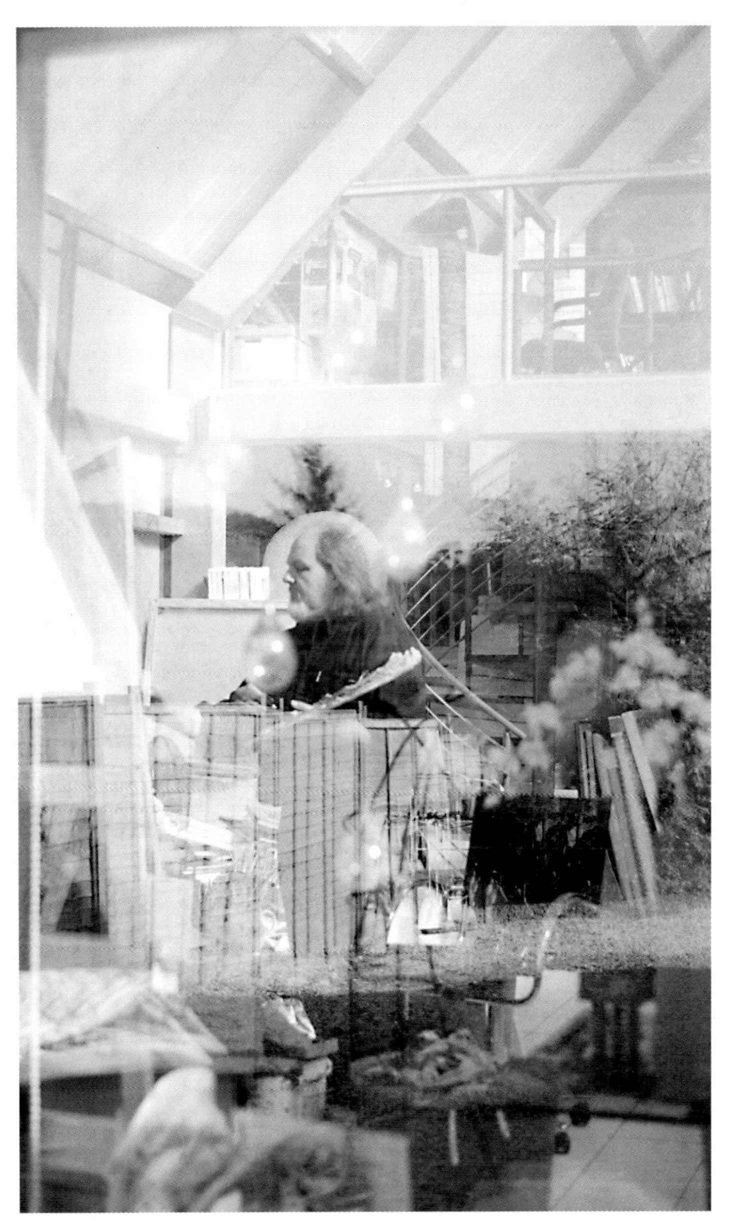

Kranenburg & Fowler Arts	Oban	2001
Queens Gallery	Dundee	2001
Torrance Gallery	Edinburgh	2002
Castle Gallery	Rothesay	2002
Kranenburg & Fowler Arts _Caledonian MacBrayne Colonsay Cruise_	Oban	2002
Ayr Gallery	London	2002
The Archway Gallery	Lochgilphead	2002
Tighnabruaich Gallery	Tighnabruaich	2002
Walker Gallery	Harrogate	2002
Kranenburg & Fowler Arts	Oban	2002

Work in many private and corporate collections throughout the world including: United Kingdom - Ireland - Germany - Spain - The Netherlands - France - Australia - Italy - Brazil - Israel - Canada - Switzerland - Austria - Luxembourg - China.

US States: Texas - Vermont - North Carolina - Florida - Pennsylvania - New Jersey - Illinois - Wisconsin - New York - Michigan - Arizona. Also collections in New York - Los Angeles - Chicago - Beverley Hills - Carmel - Connecticut.

UK: Bank of Scotland - Inland Revenue, Edinburgh - The High Court, Edinburgh - Cairn Energy - Trinity Gas - Argyll & Lomond Health Trust - Deutsche Morgan Grenfell, London - British Opthalmic Association - Bank of New York - Woburn Abbey - Sanderson Young.

media

BBC North

HKTV - China

Oban FM

BBC Cambridge

Anglia TV

Film of John Lowrie Morrison - Scottish Masters series produced by STV

DVD film - John Lowrie Morrison - 'I know where I am going' produced by MitchellMcGloneFilms

The Oban Times

The Glasgow Express

The Glasgow Herald

The Daily Express

Life and Work

John Lowrie Morrison:

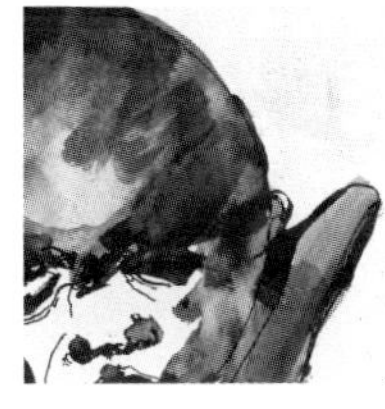

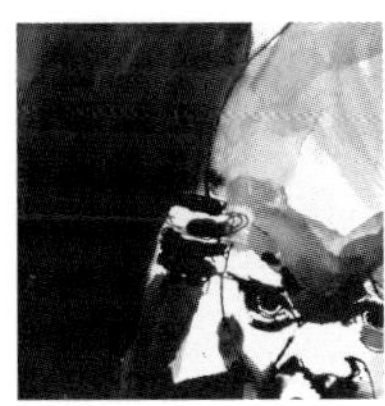

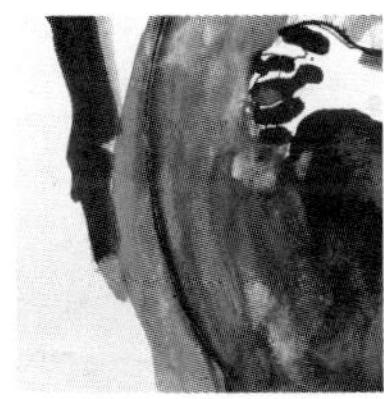
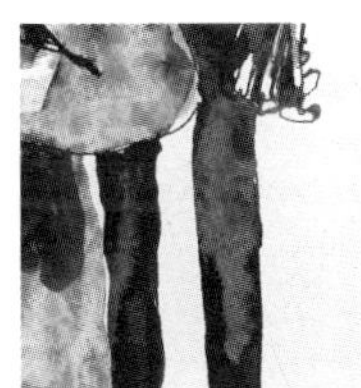

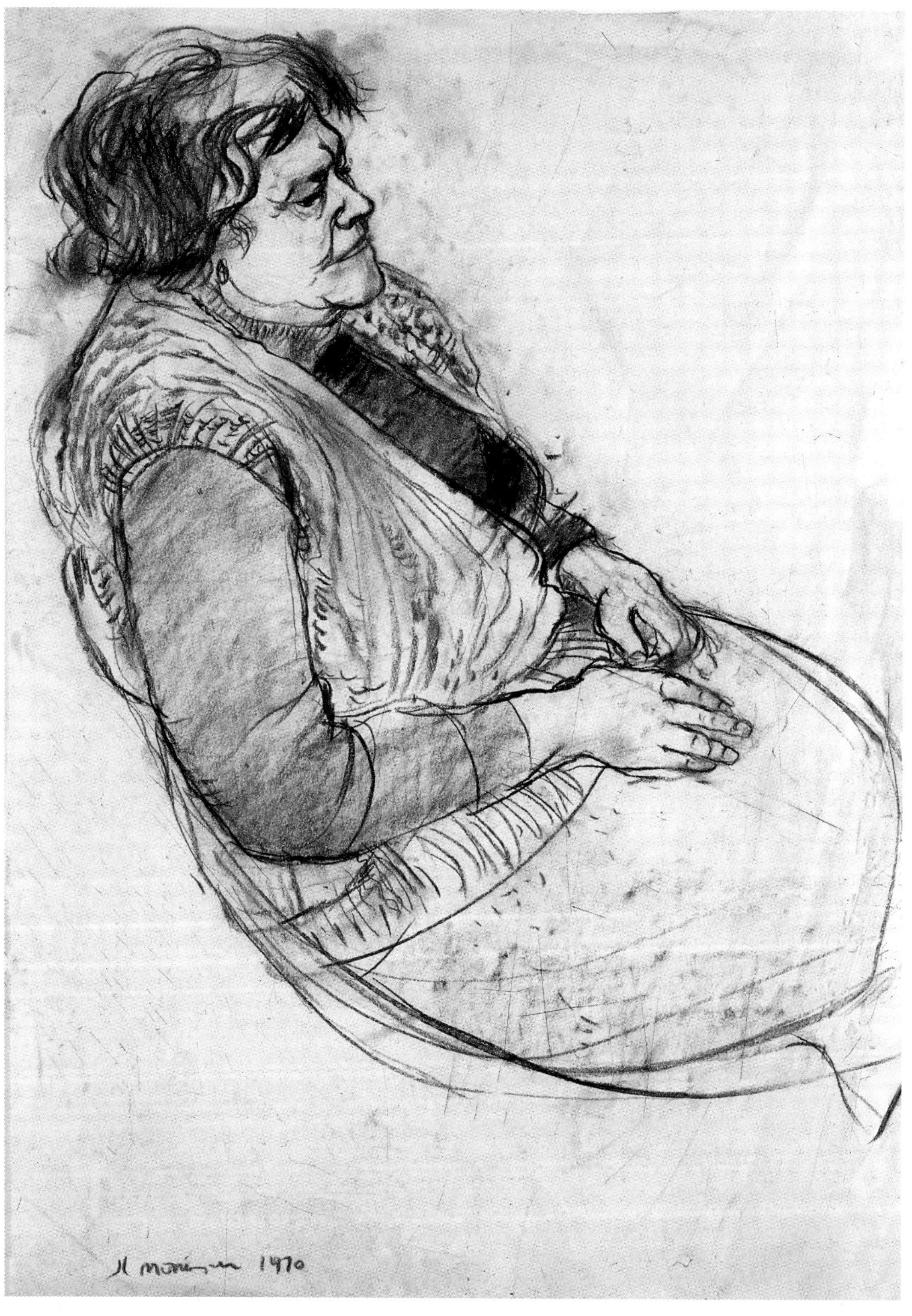

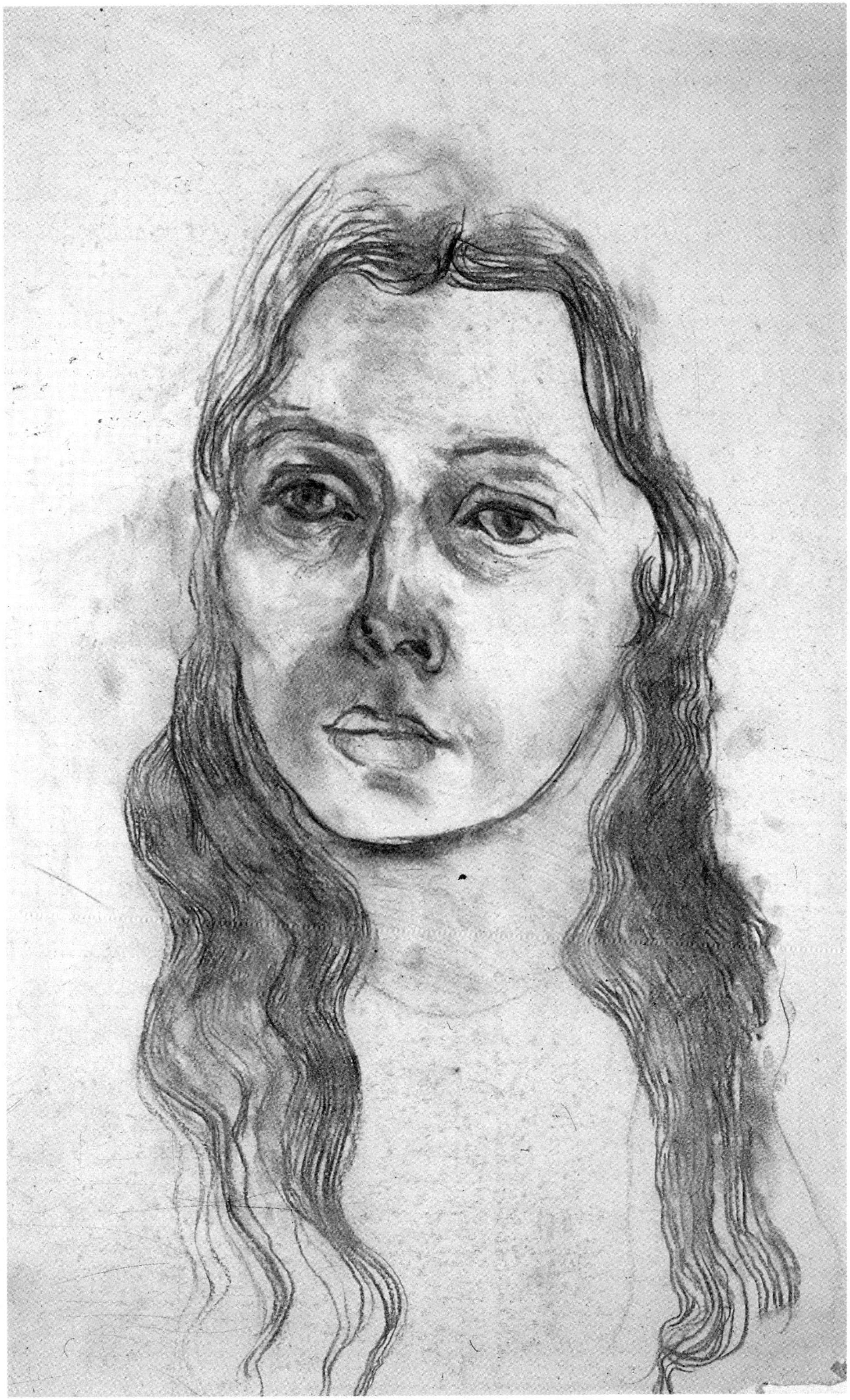

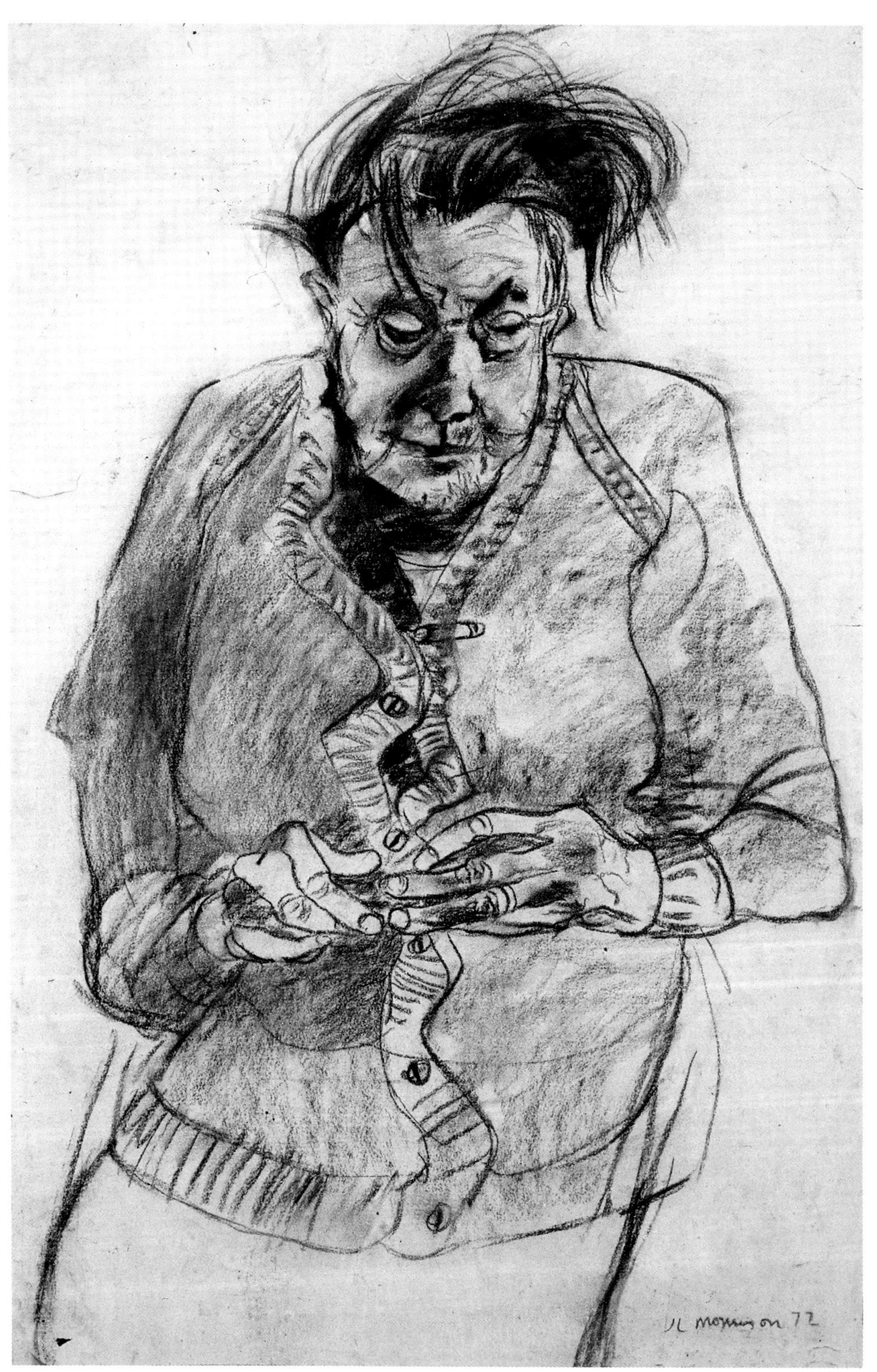

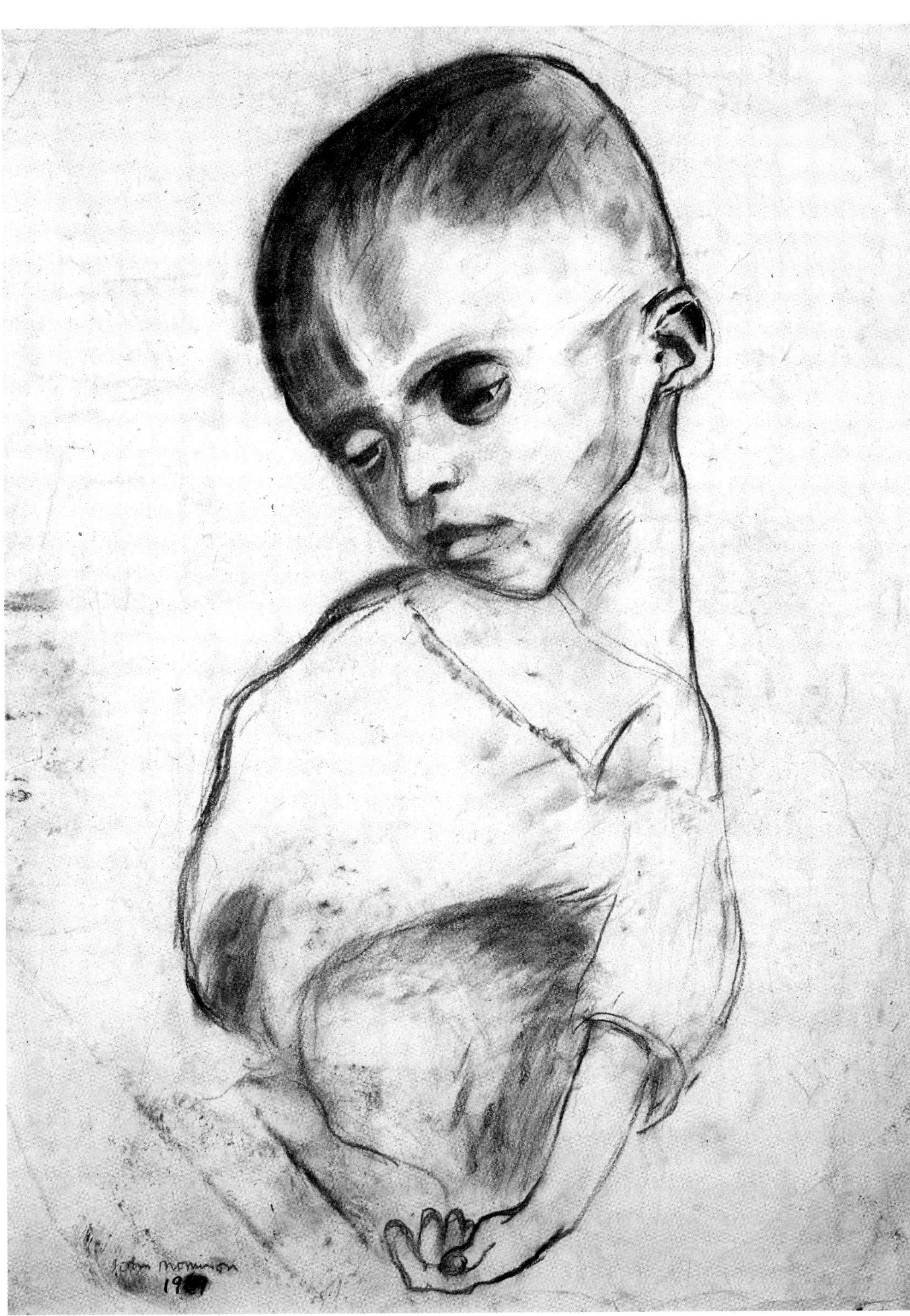

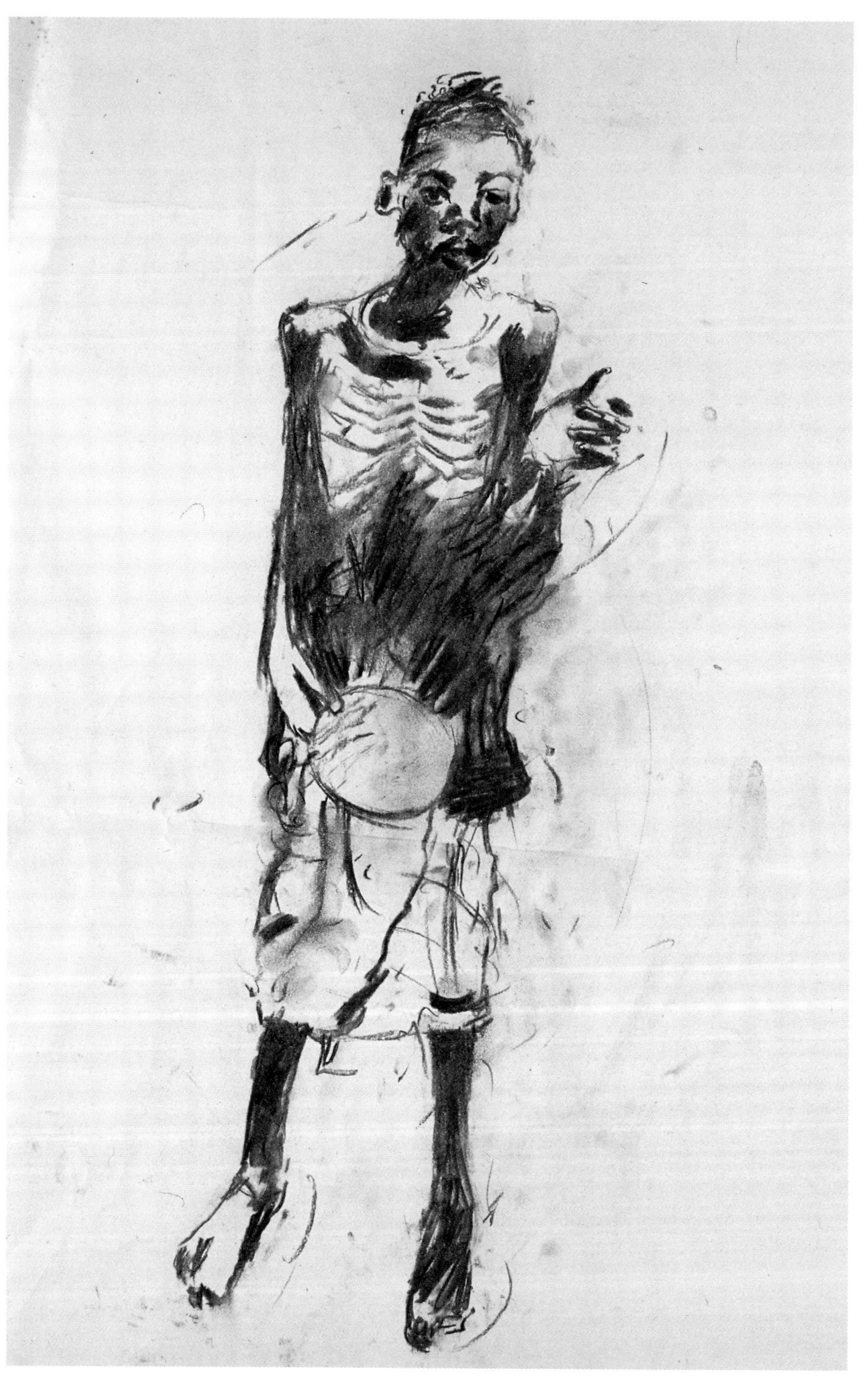

No food - Biafra 1970   charcoal   30 x 20

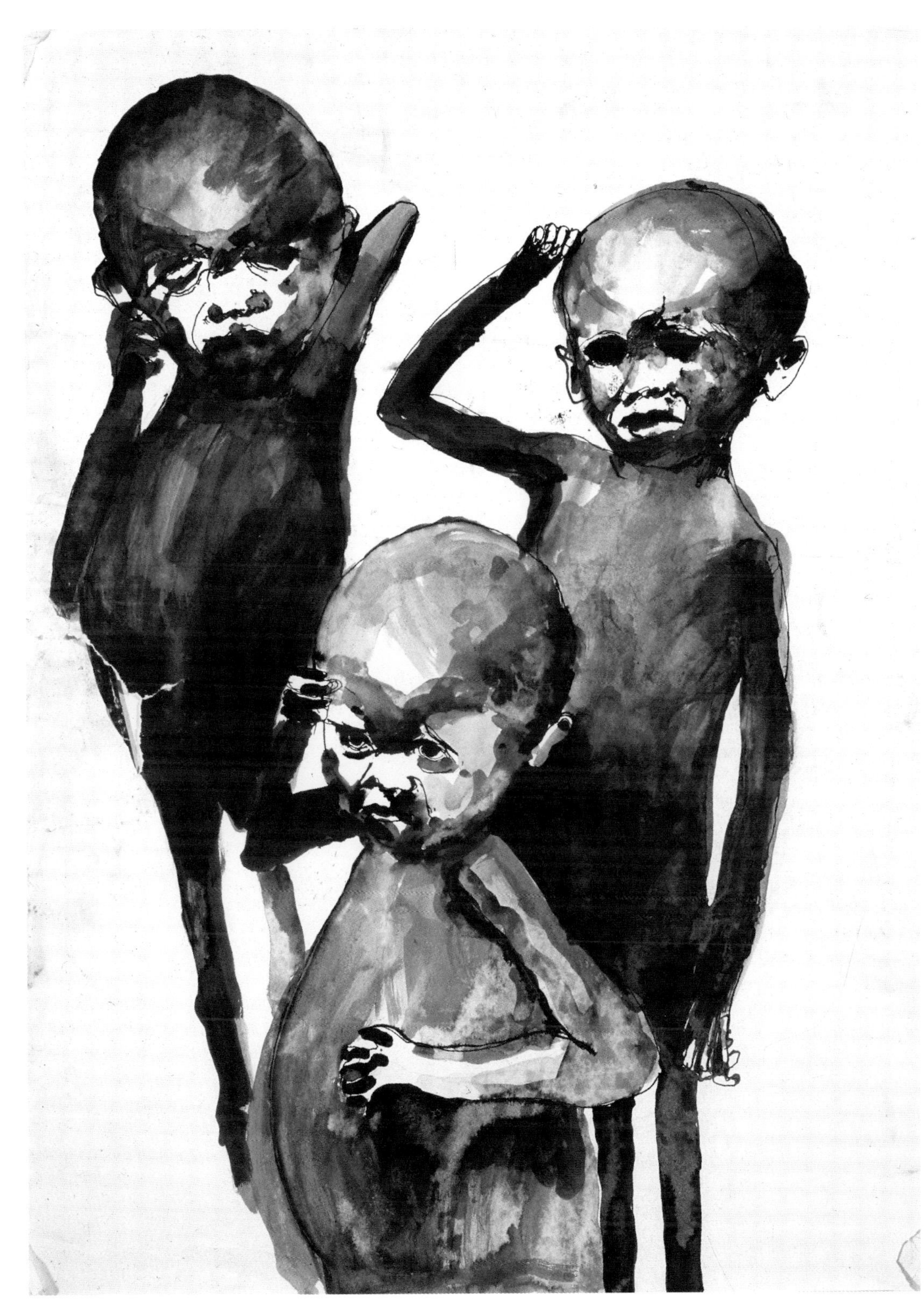

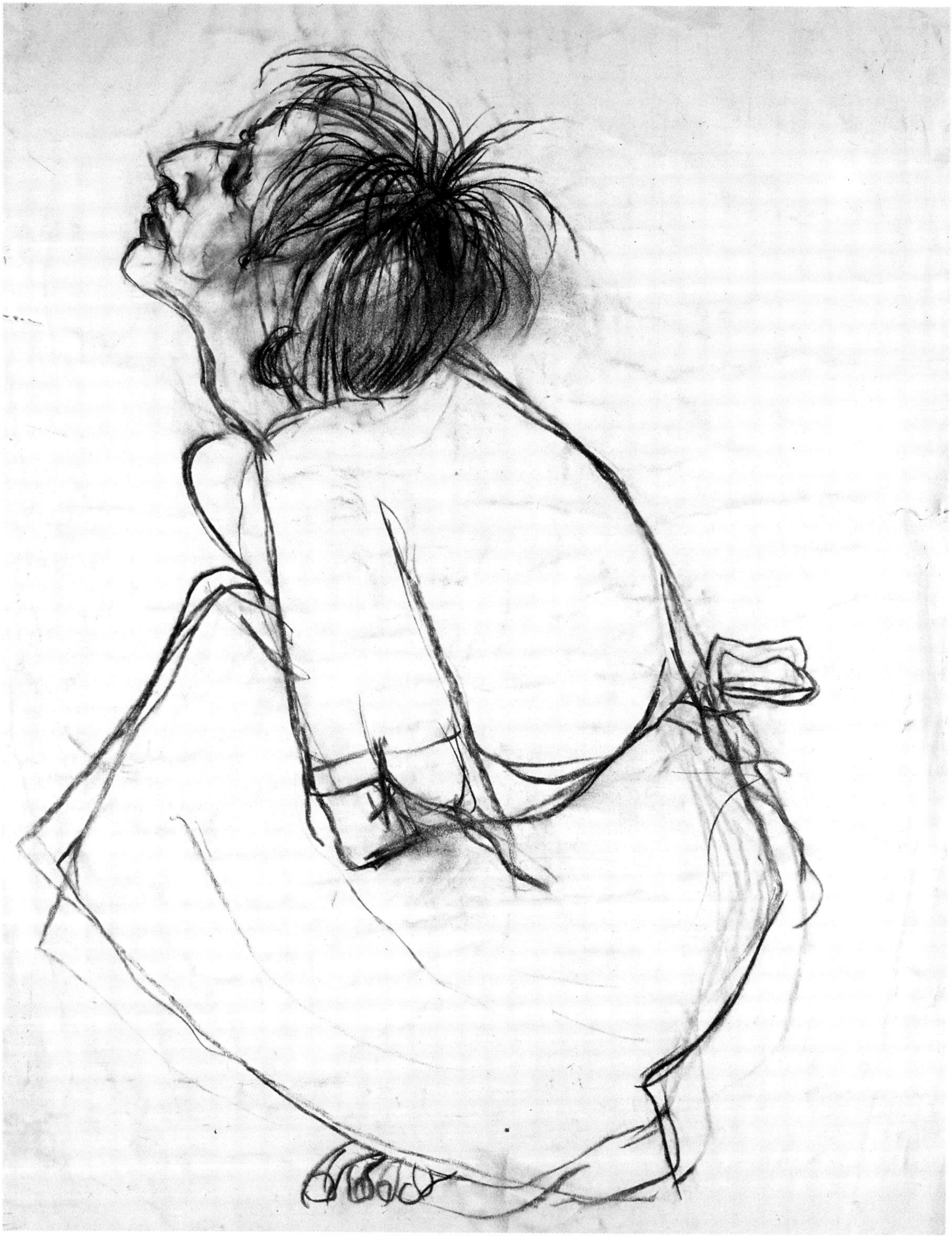

'Enough'   1970   charcoal   30 x 20"

James   1971   charcoal   40 x 30"

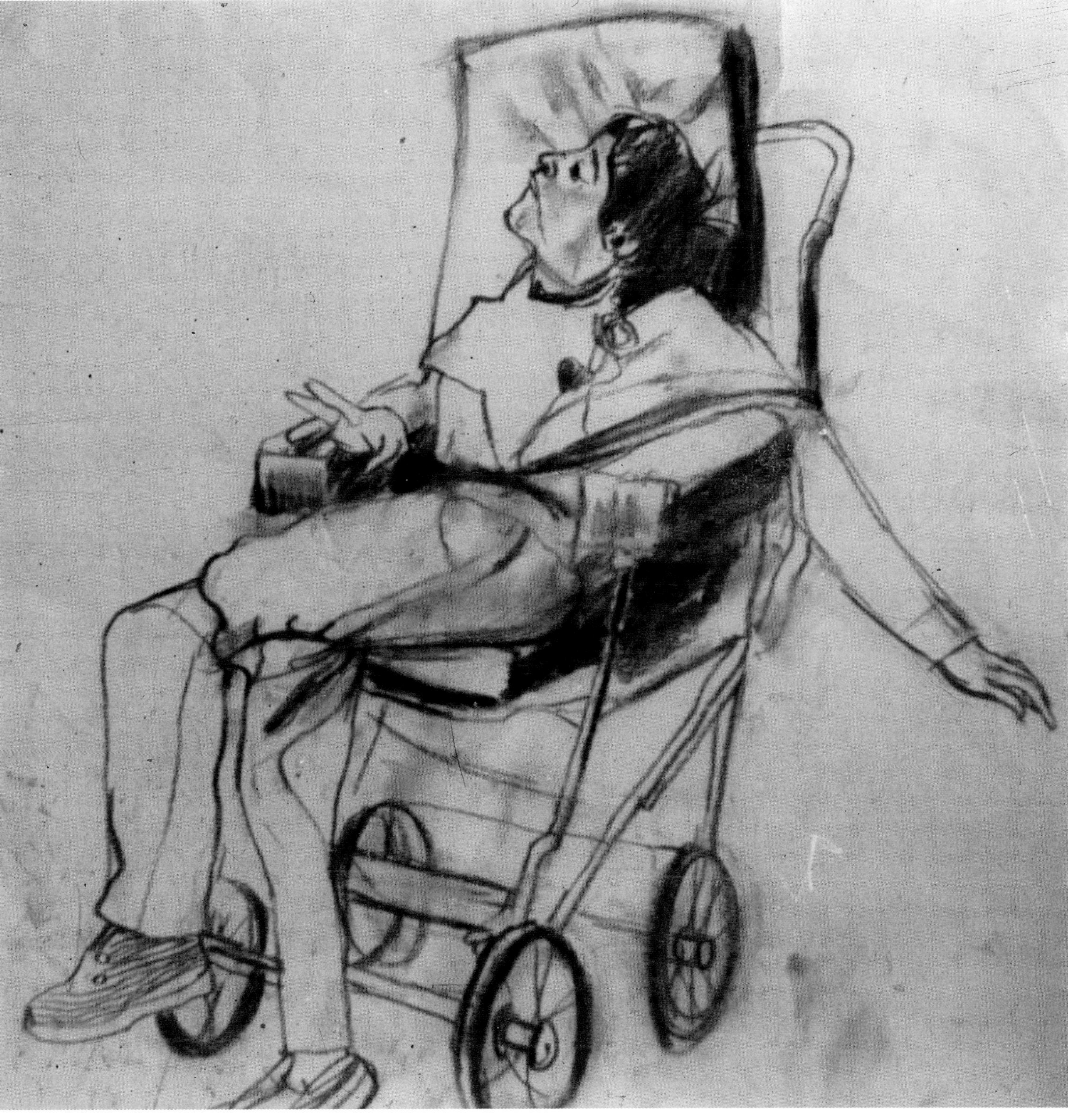

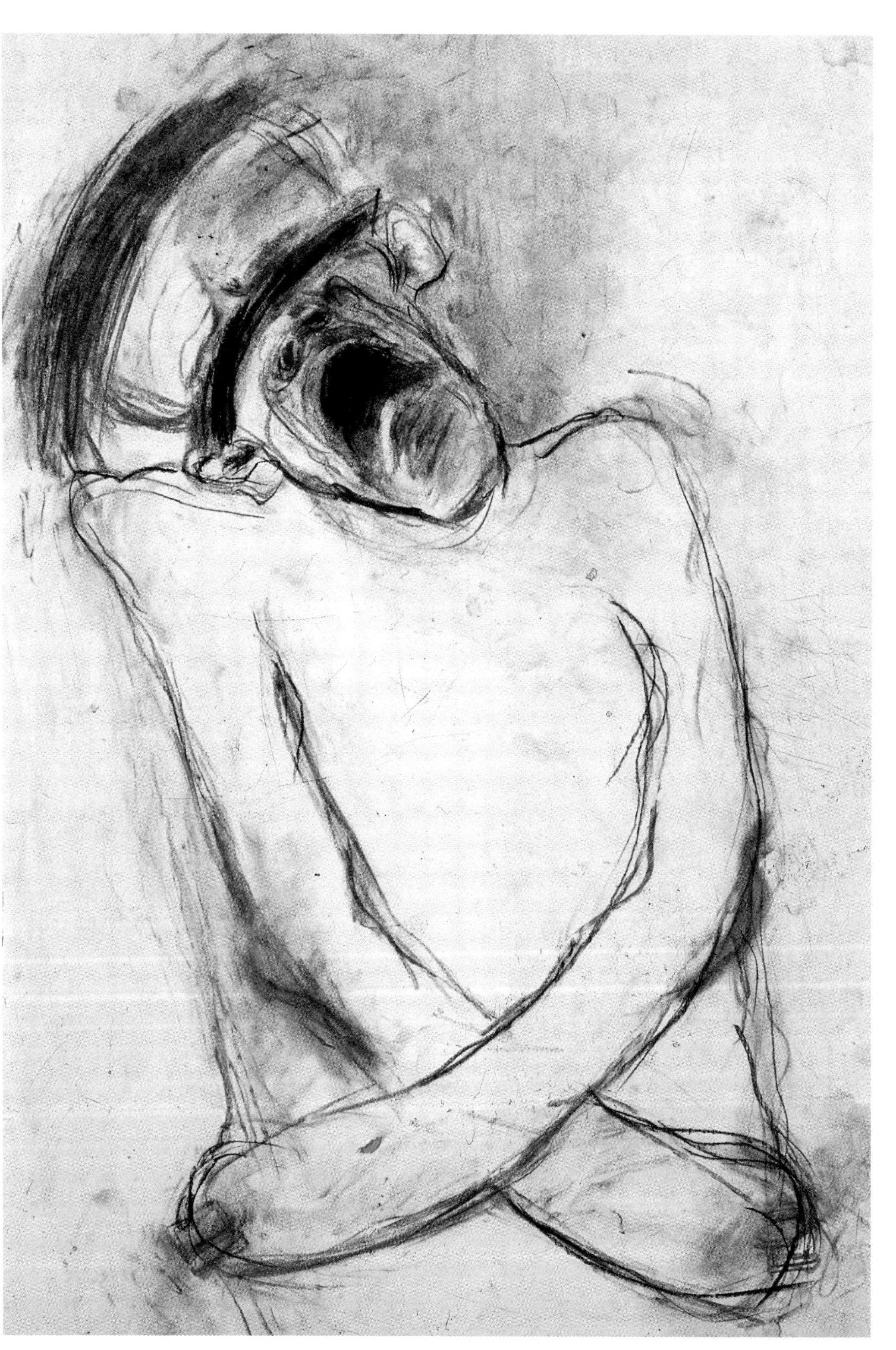

No escape - except through Christ   1971   charcoal   40 x 30"

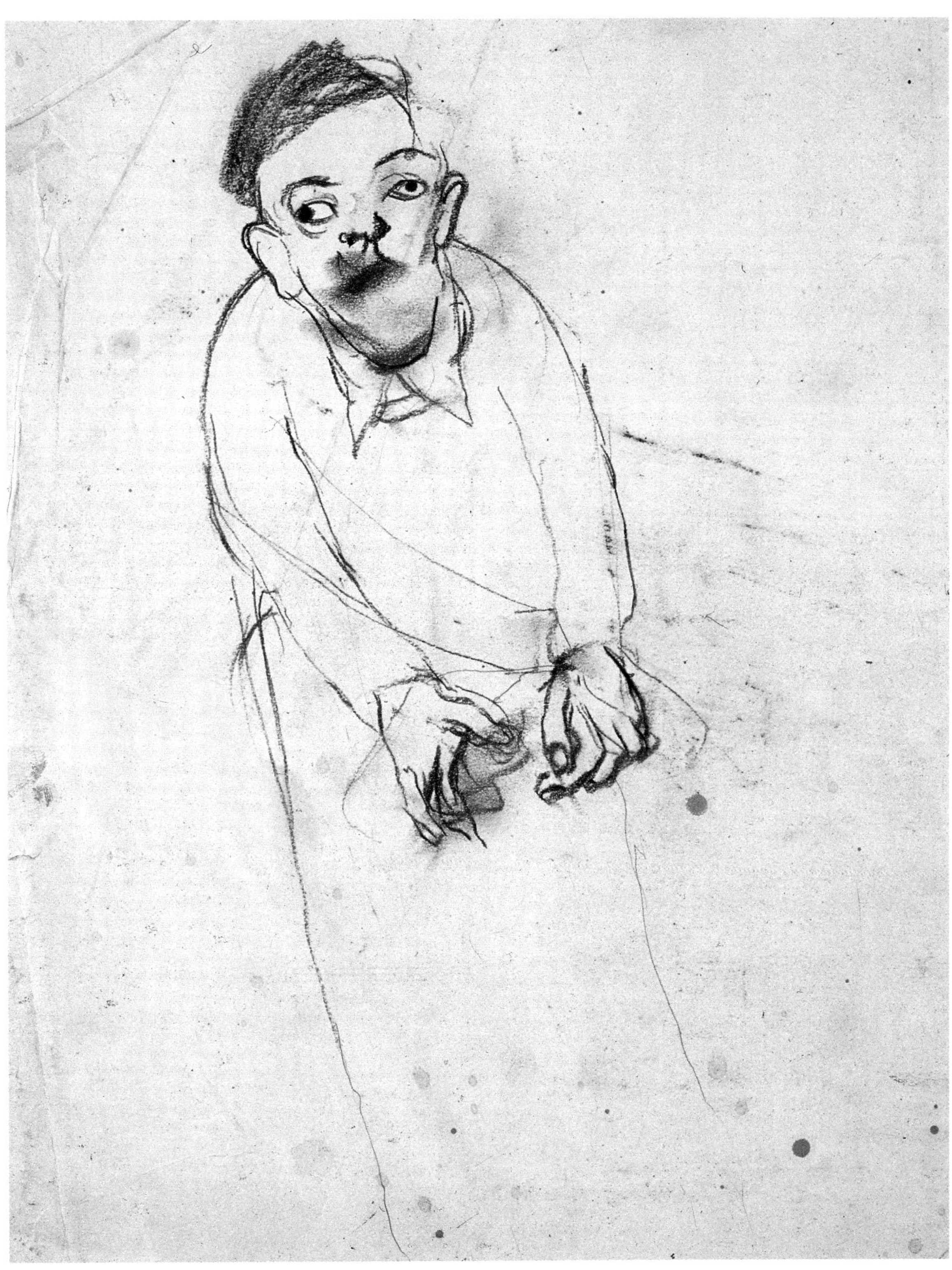

John Lowrie Morrison:

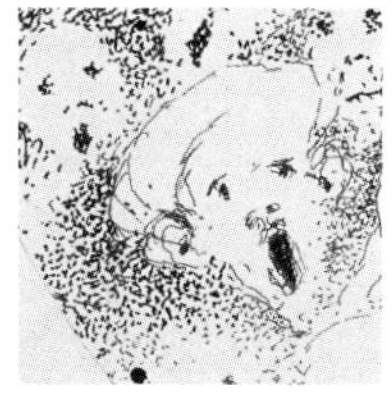

1991

pen

20 x 16"

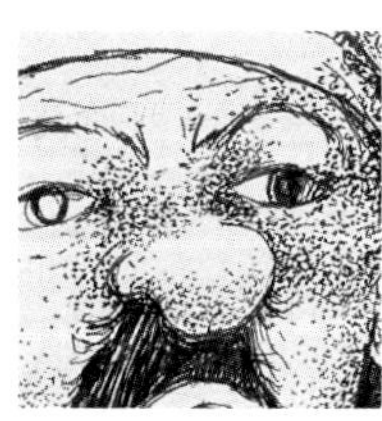

The oil painting 'Christ carrying the Cross' wasn't completed until 2002 (see page 75) but it is obvious that the idea had been developing in John's mind for some time. This study, eleven years old, shows John's fascination with the subject. He is pleased to be 'free of financial constraints' so that he can explore biblical imagery and use religious subjects for inspiration. The painting is significantly different from the sketch, most notably perhaps in the depiction of the faces of murdered children surrounding Christ. The idea of Christ carrying this burden as part of the sins of the world (the Cross) grew out of recent events in England, and the suffering of children in wartime (particularly Bosnia).

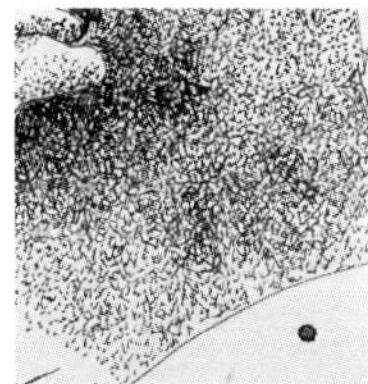

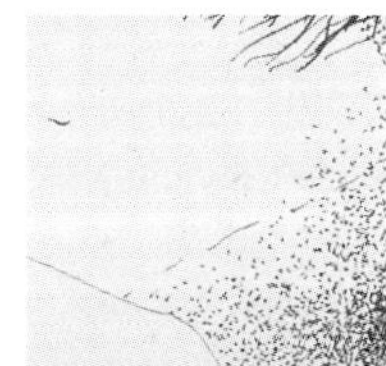

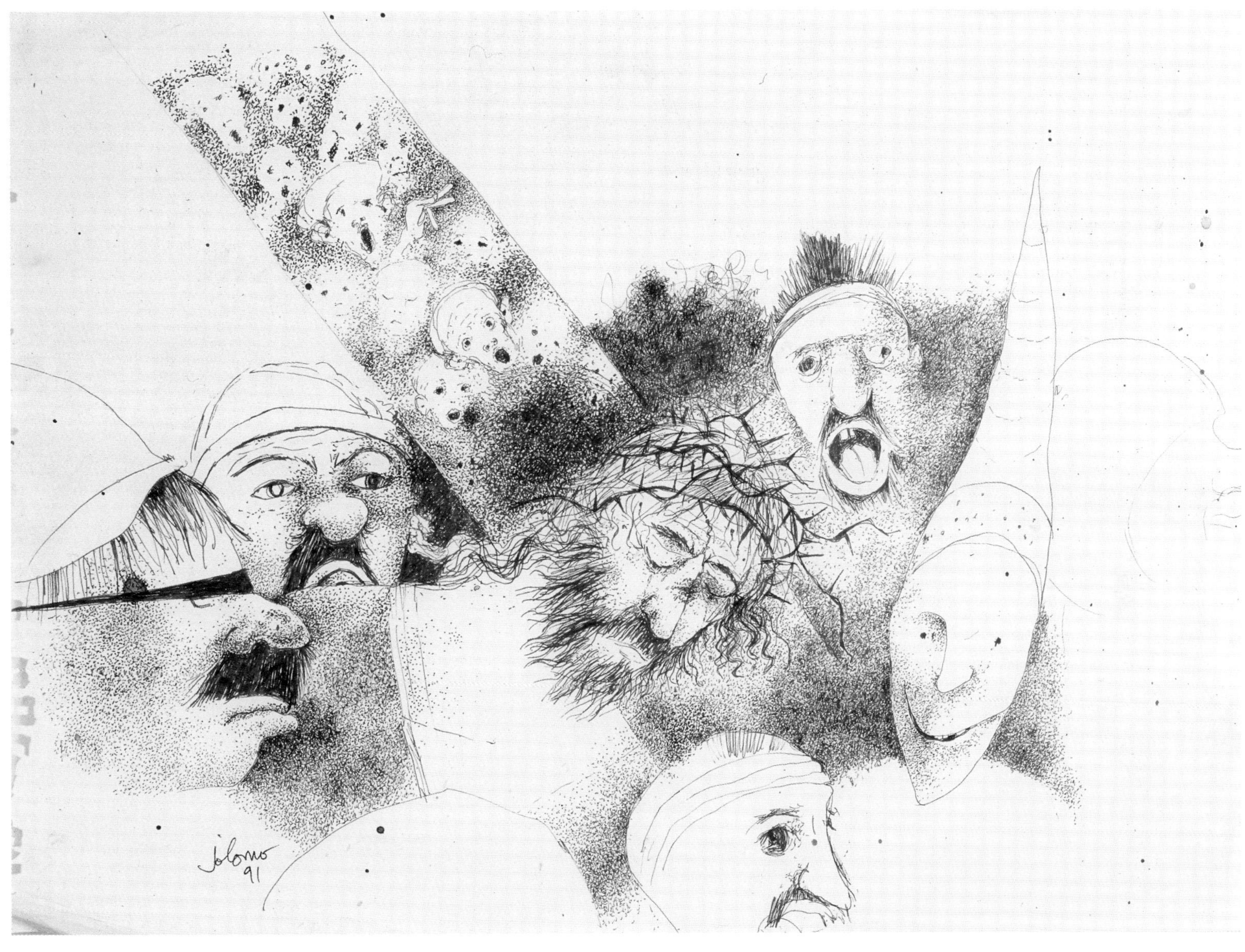

John Lowrie Morrison:

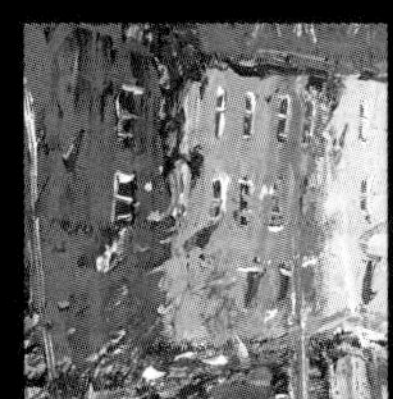

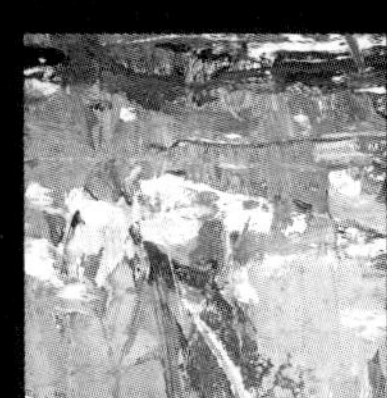

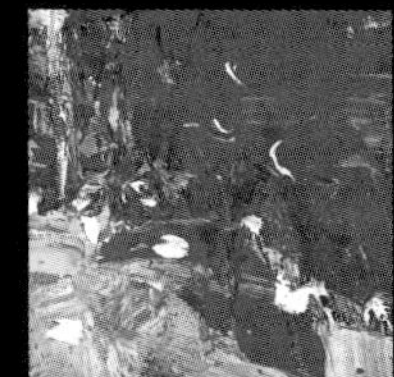

the Colour of life: page 44

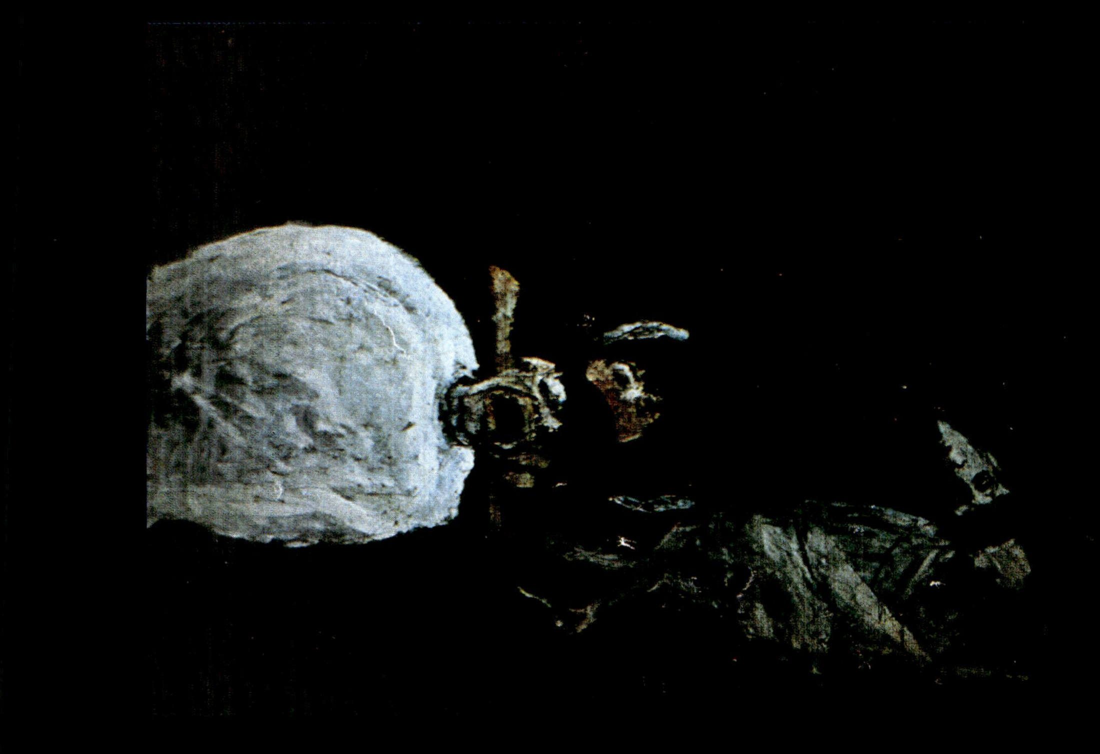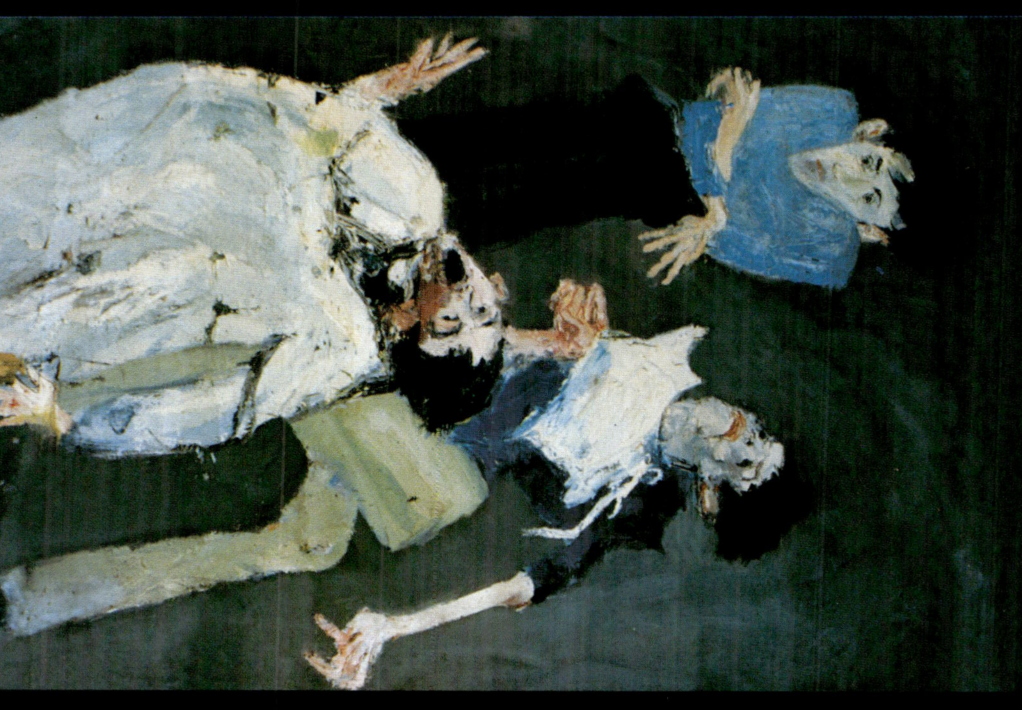

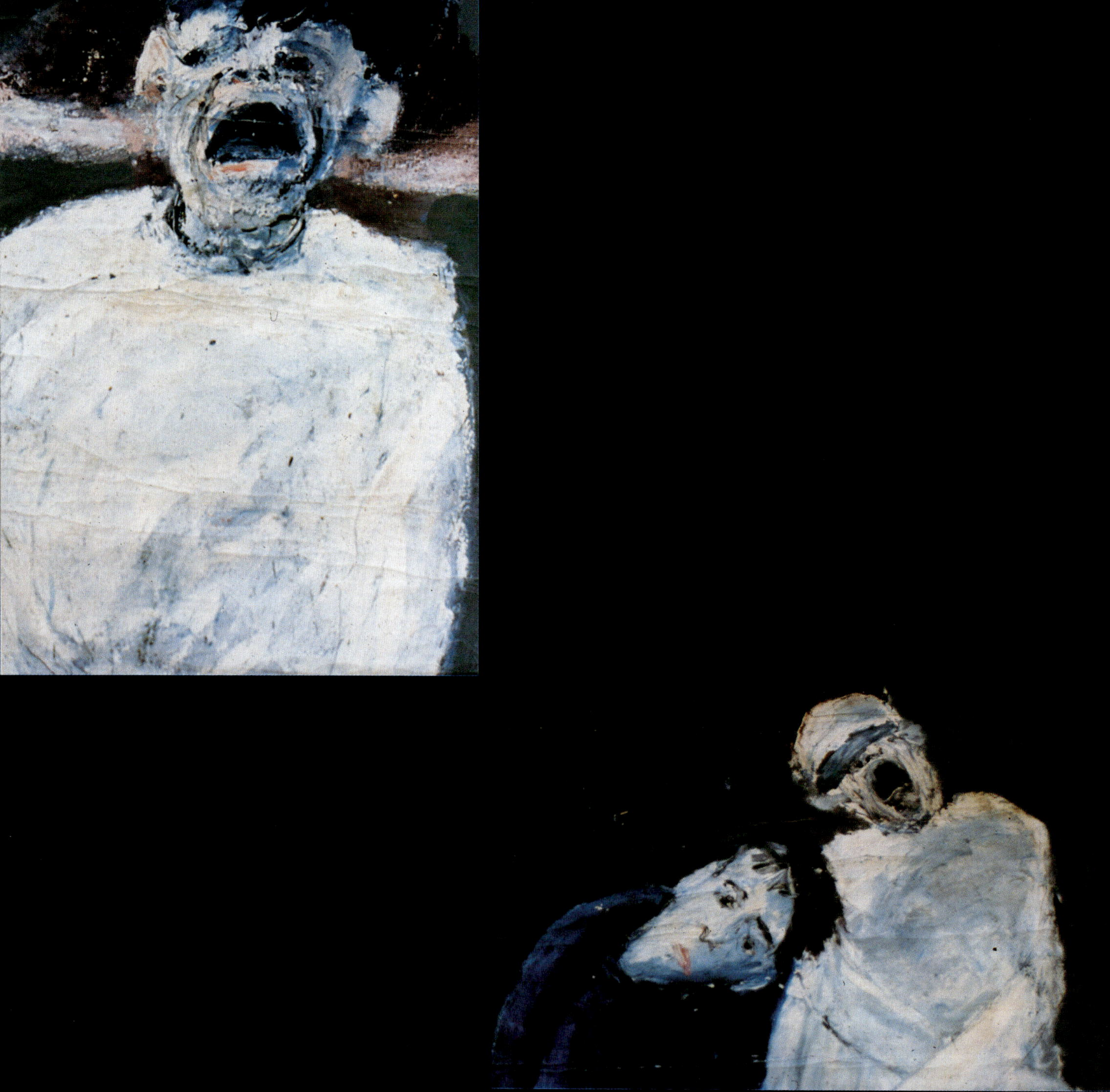

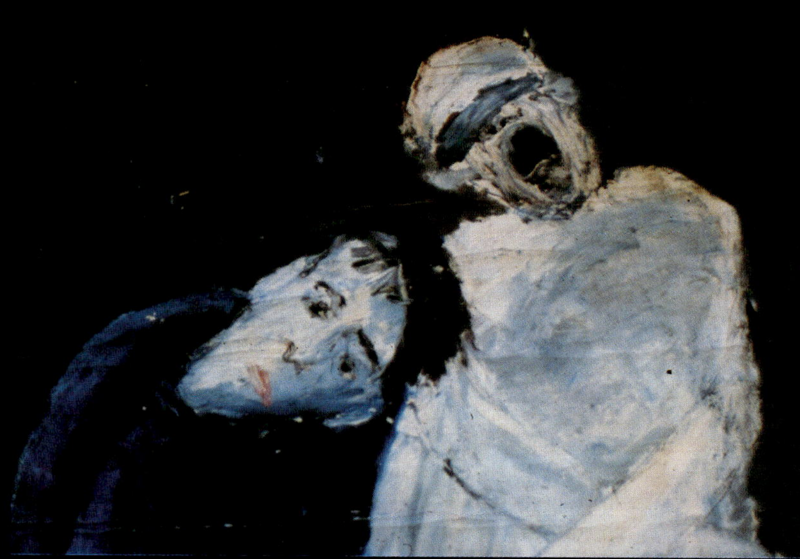

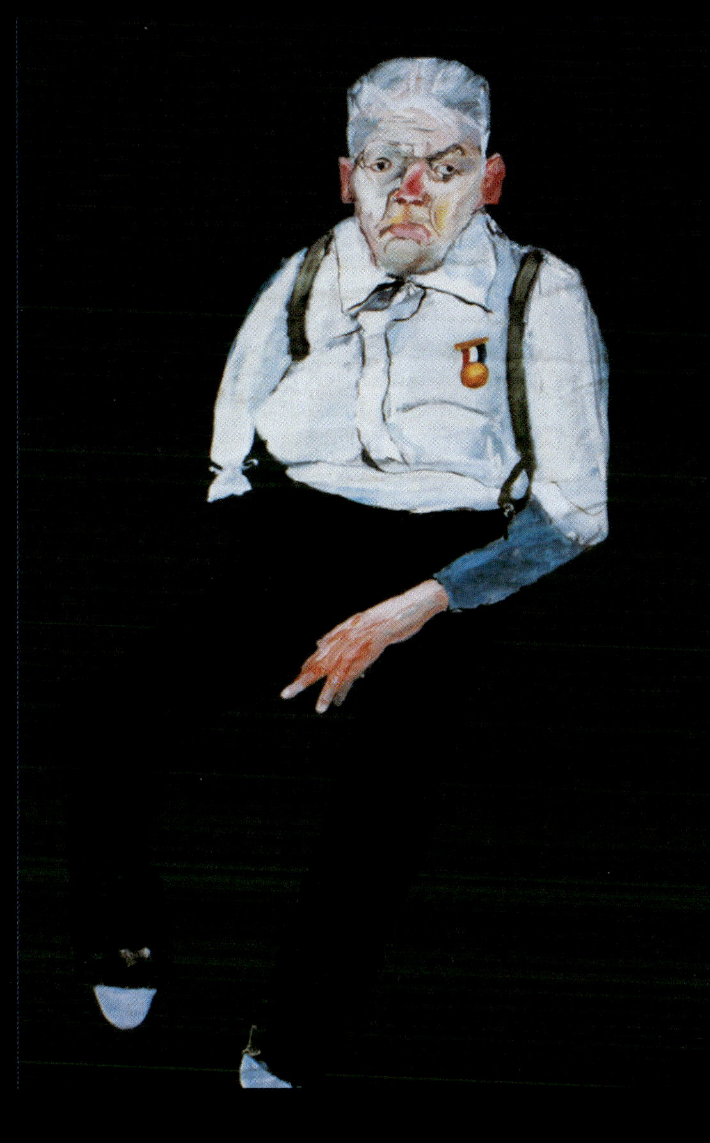
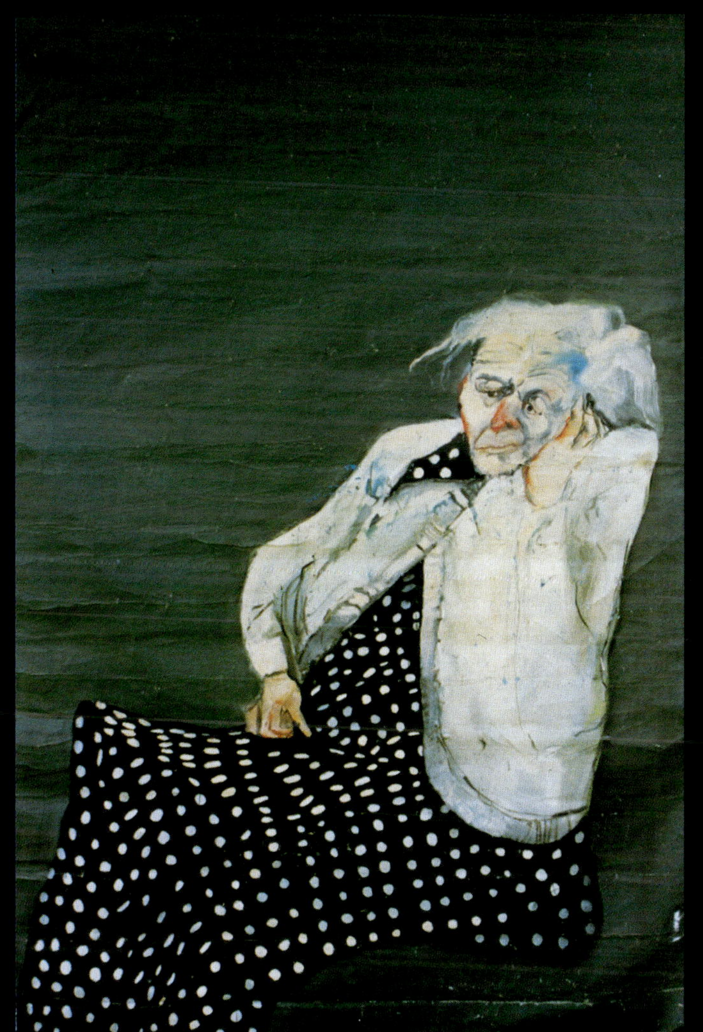

War Heroes   dyptych 1972   oil on canvas   8' x 10'

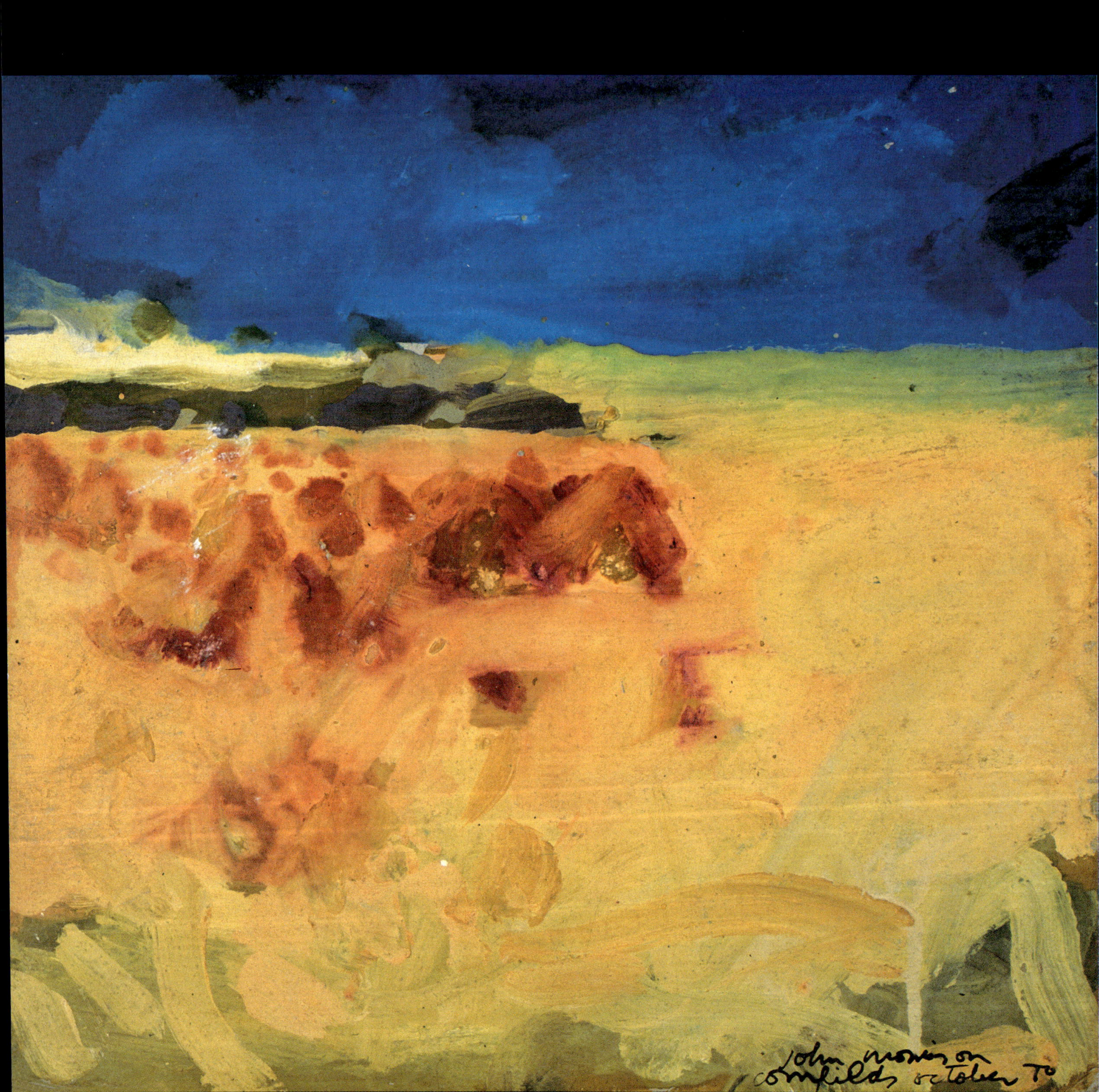

John Morrison
cornfields october 70

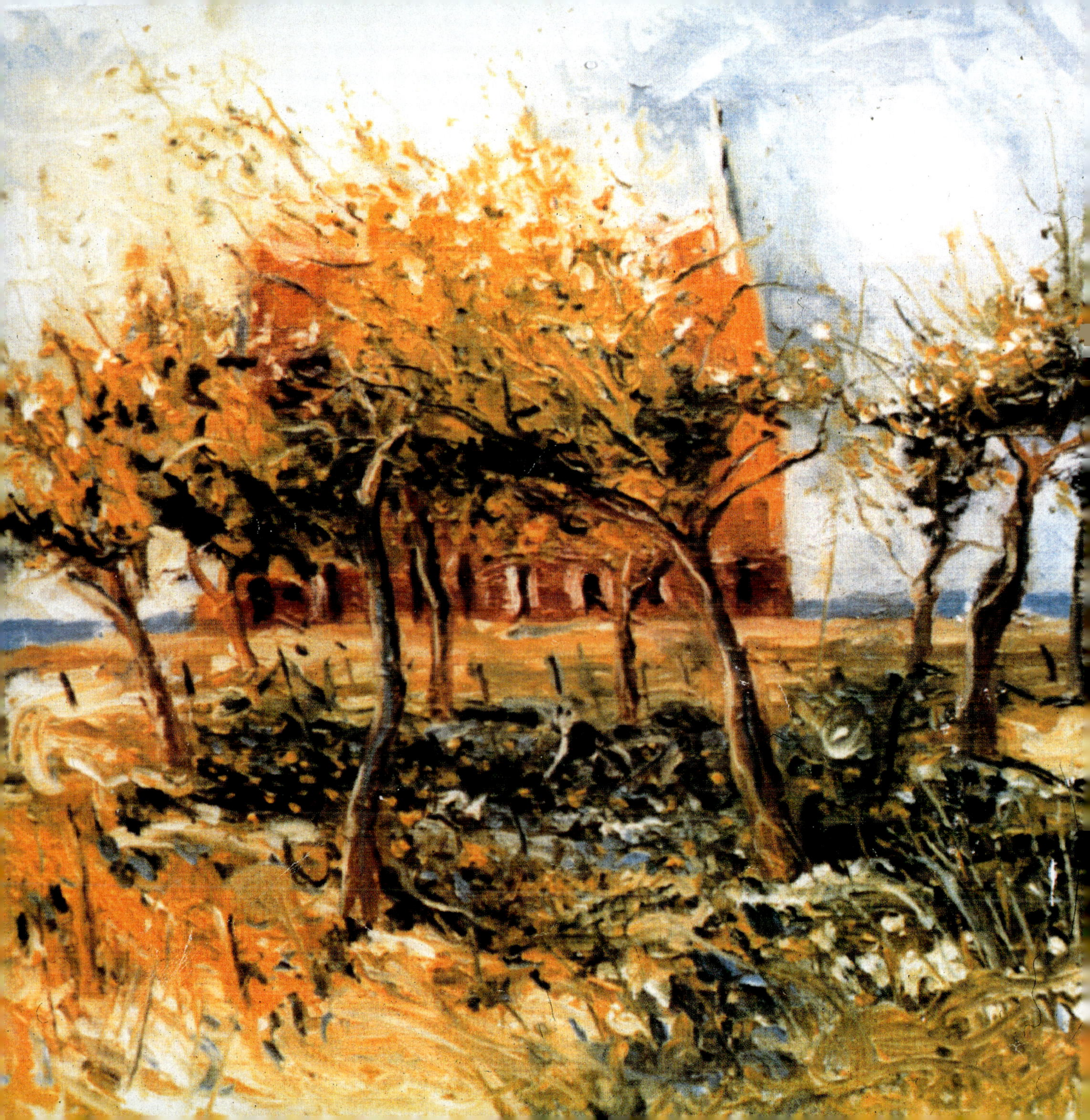

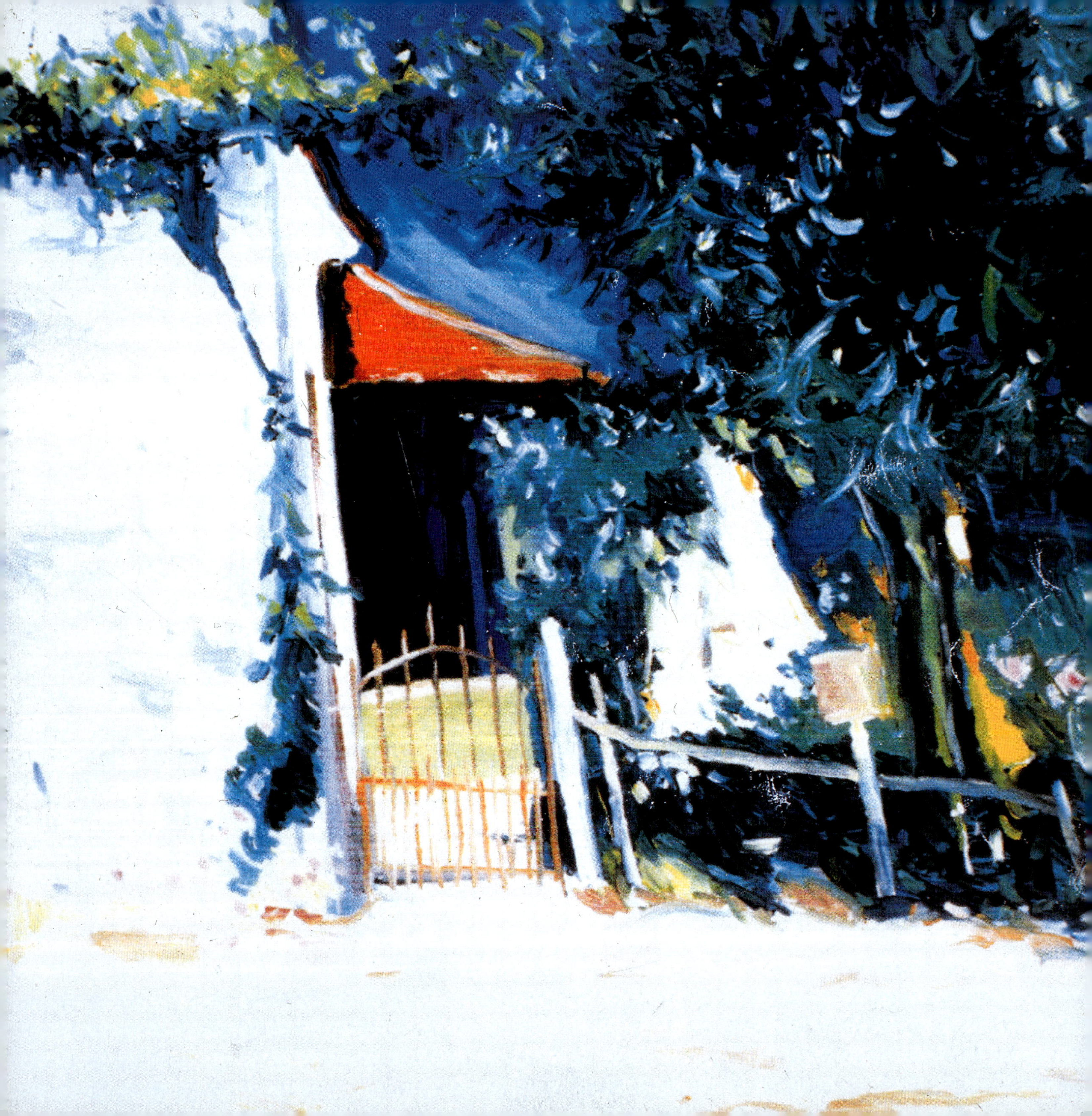

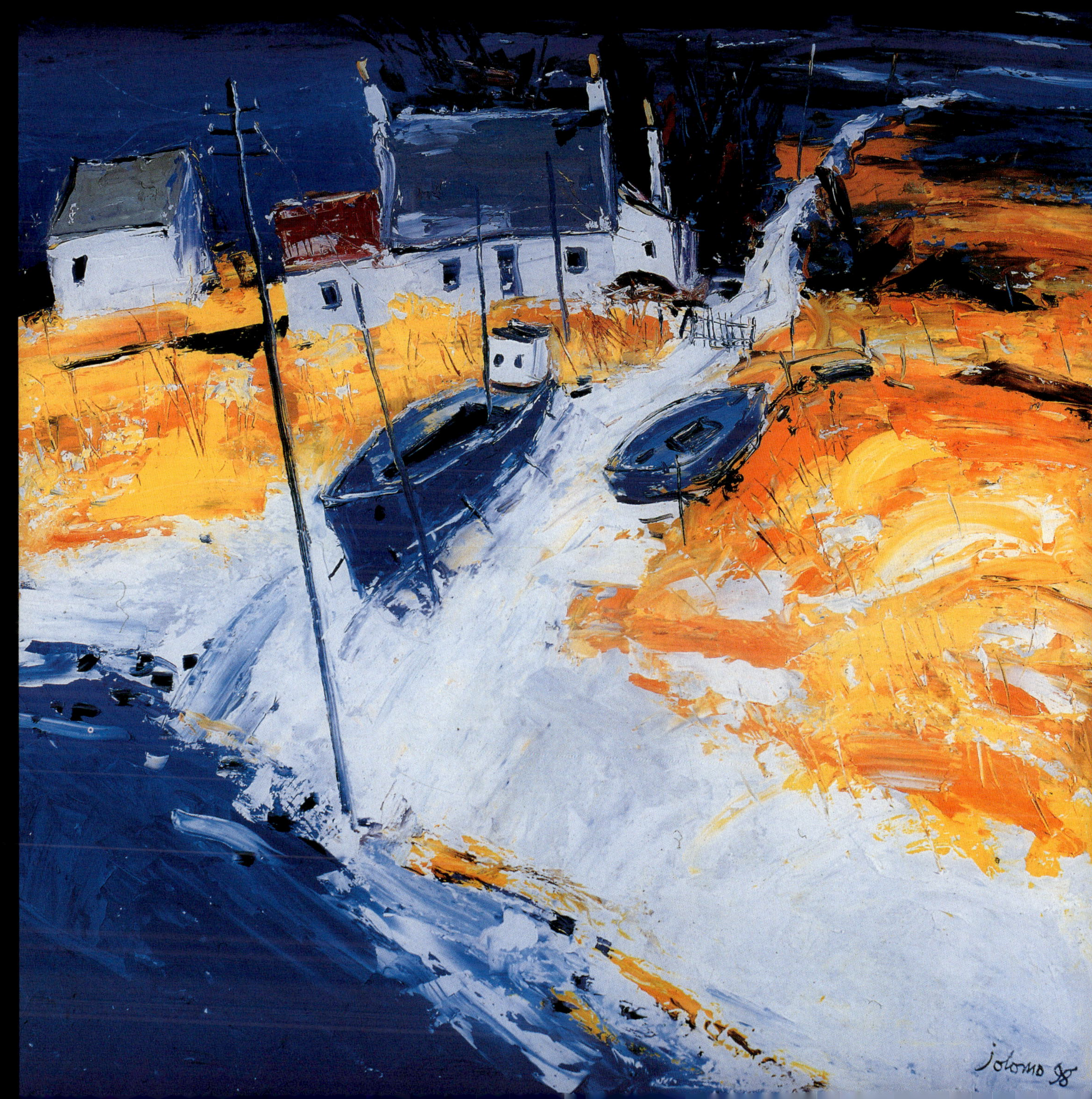

Croft by the Shore, Isle of Harris   1998   oil   30 x 30"

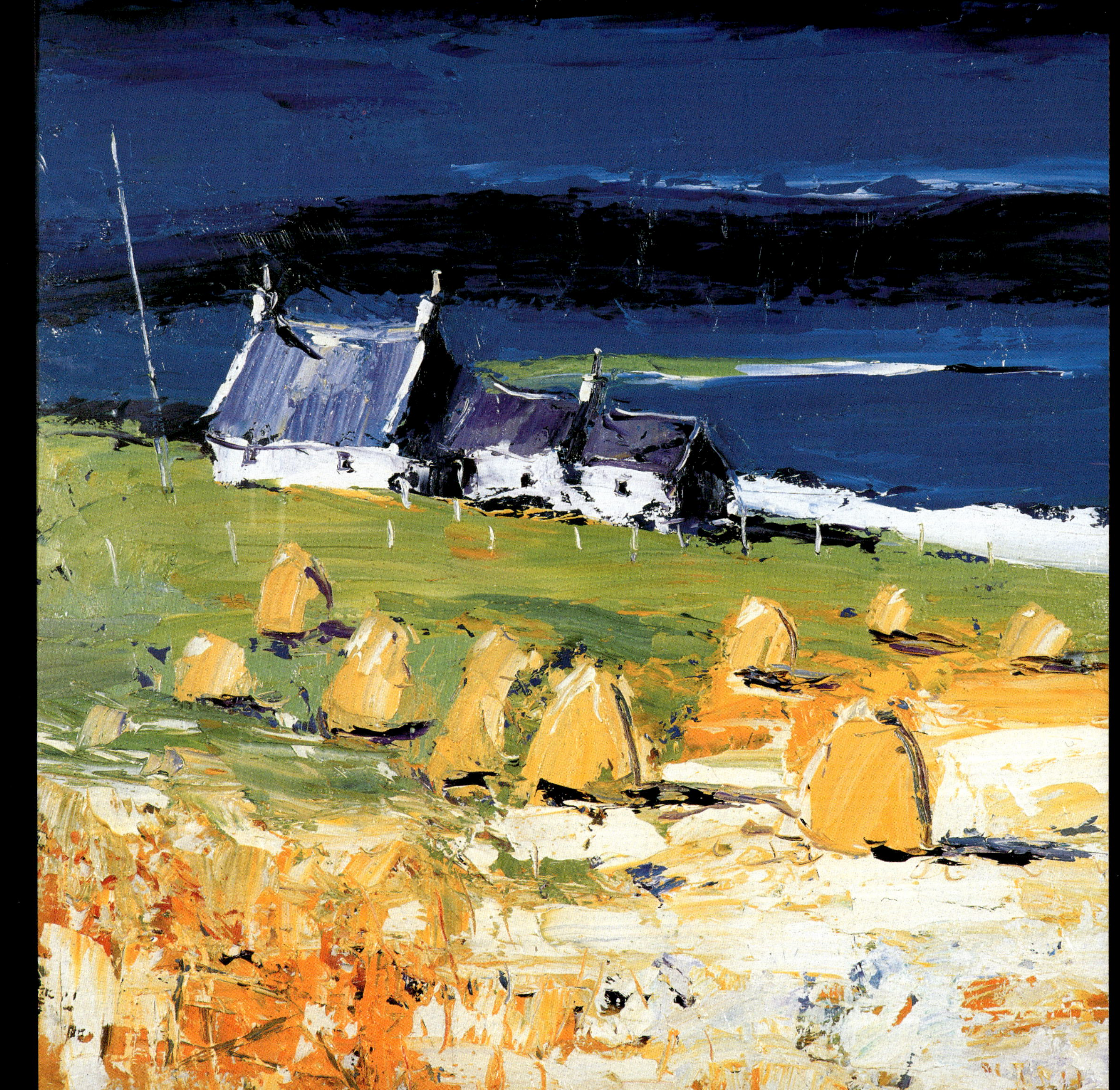

Haystacks, Iona 1999   oil   30x30

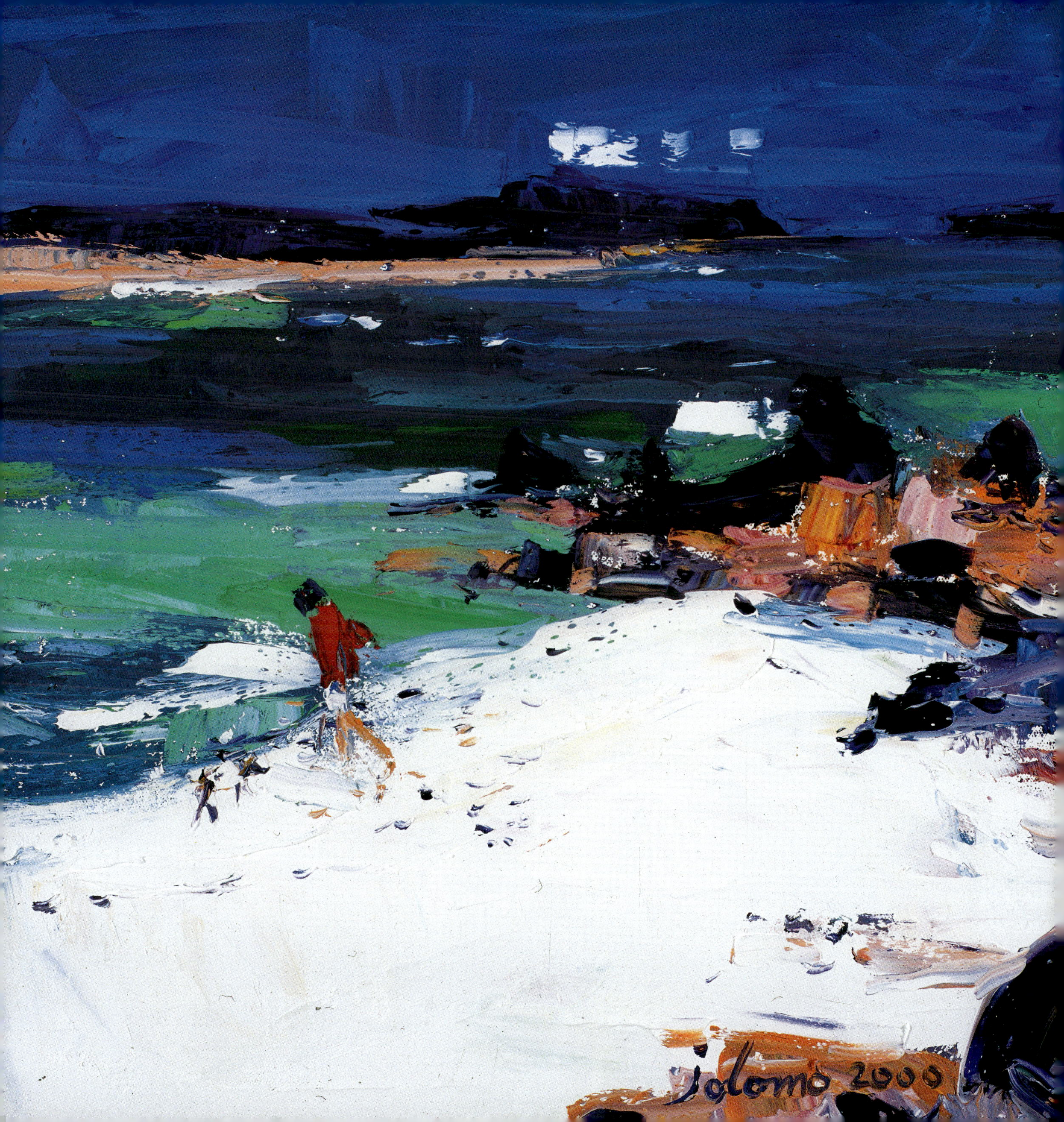

Jolomo 2000

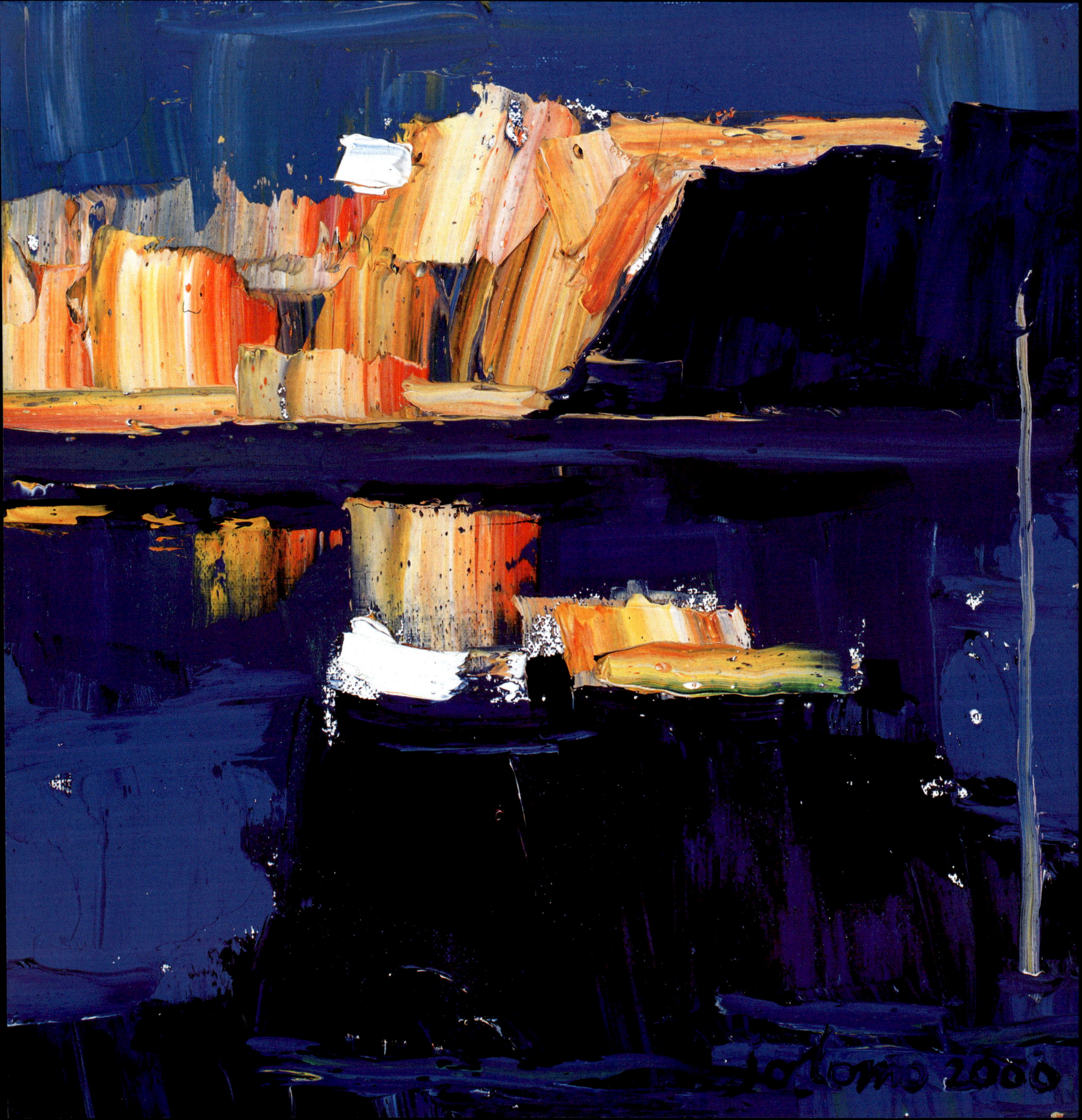

Sunset, Carsaig - Mull   2000   oil   12" x 12"

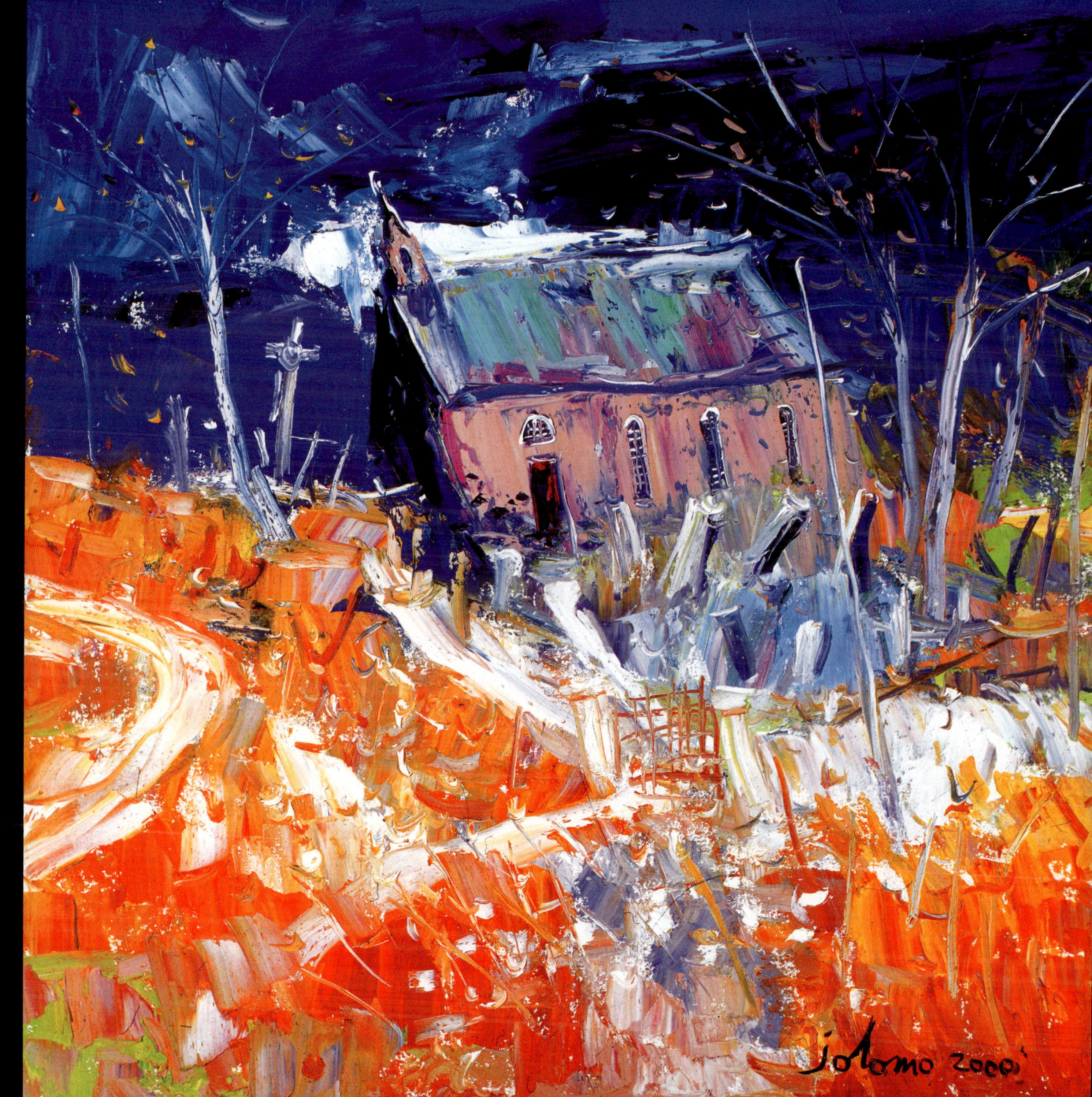
Wild Day, Kilninian Church, Torloisk Mull   2000   oil   30 x 30"

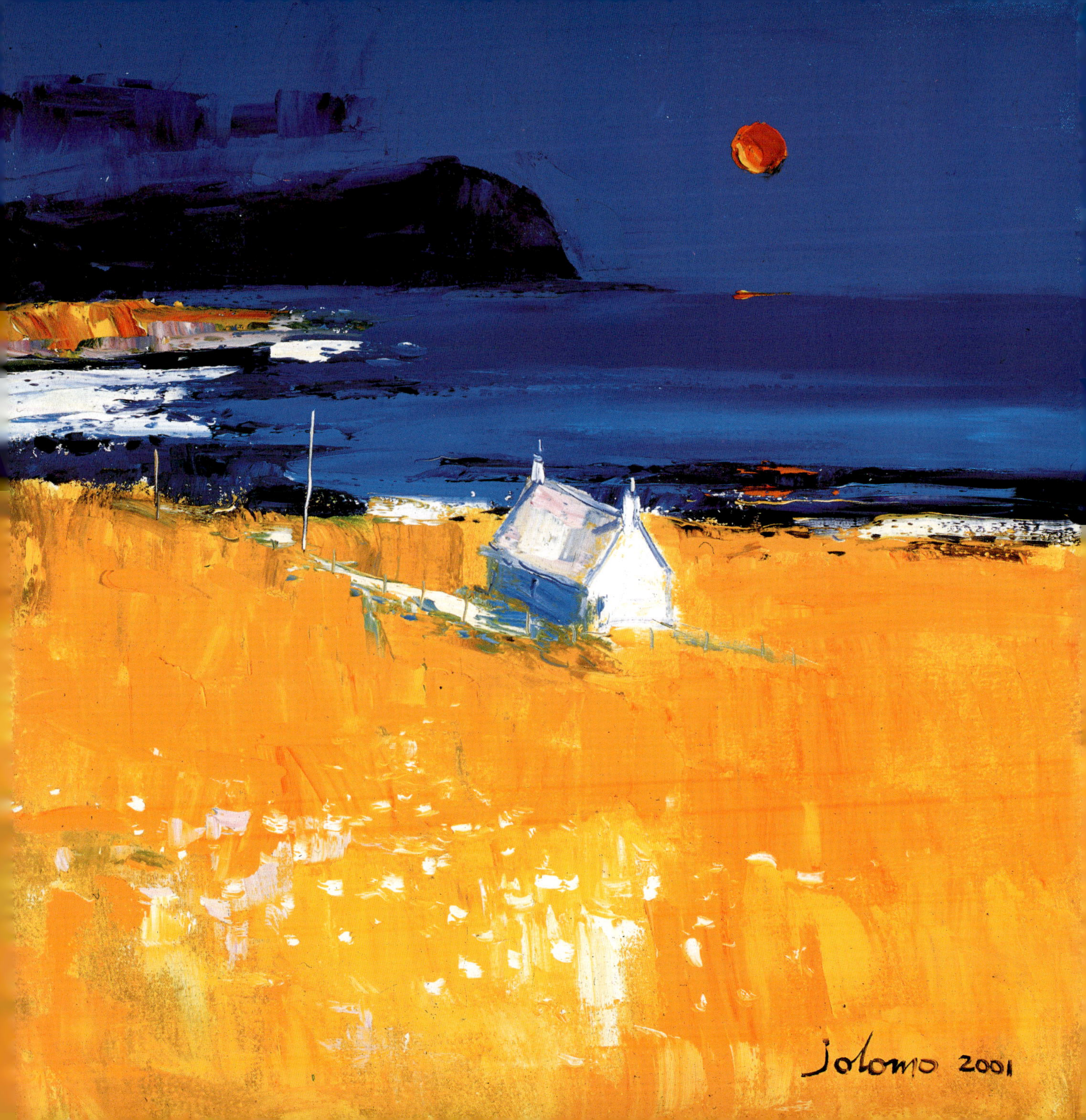

Jolomo 2001

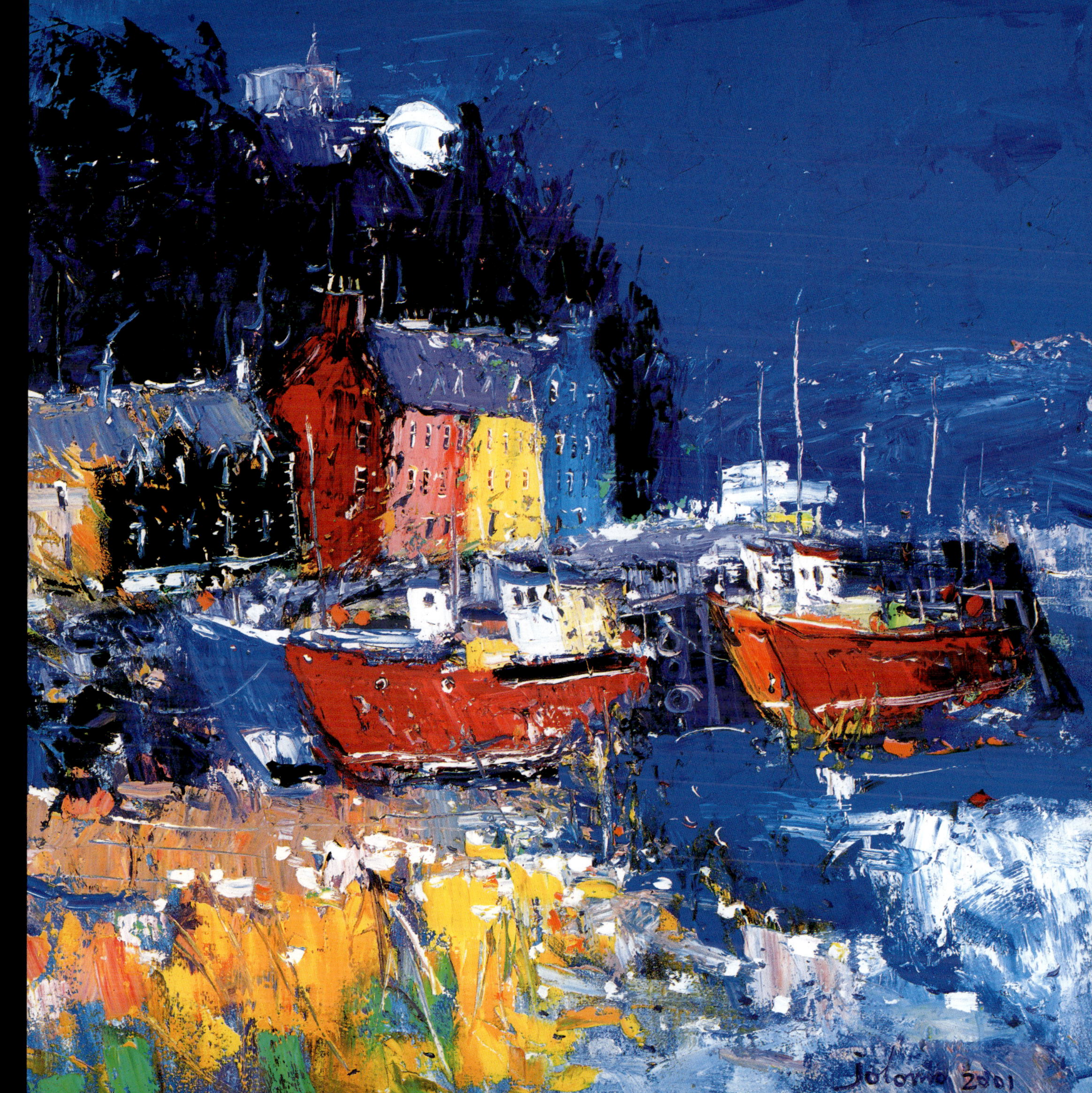

Moonrise and Fishing Boats, Tobermory   2001   oil   24 x 24"

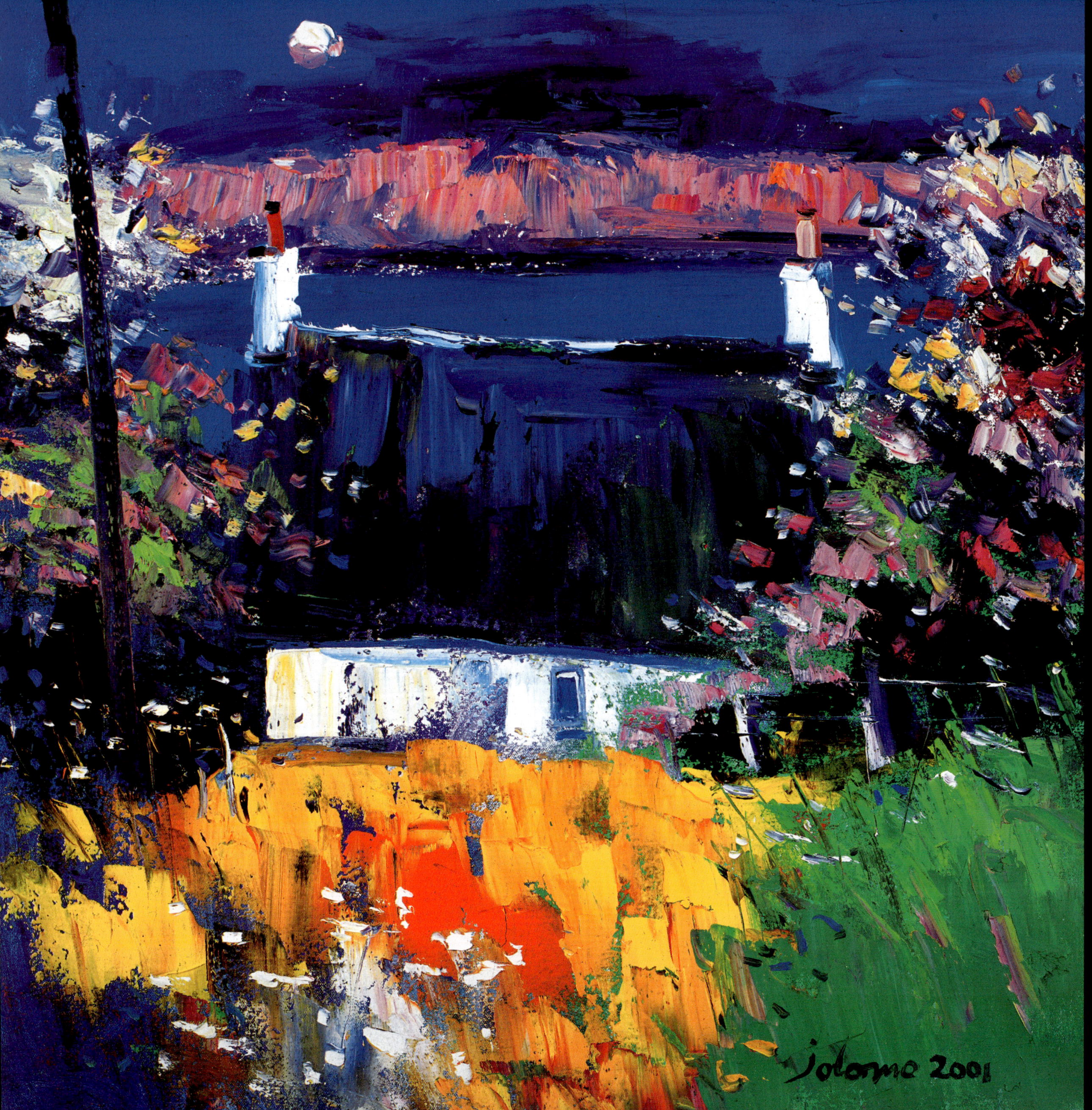
jolomo 2001

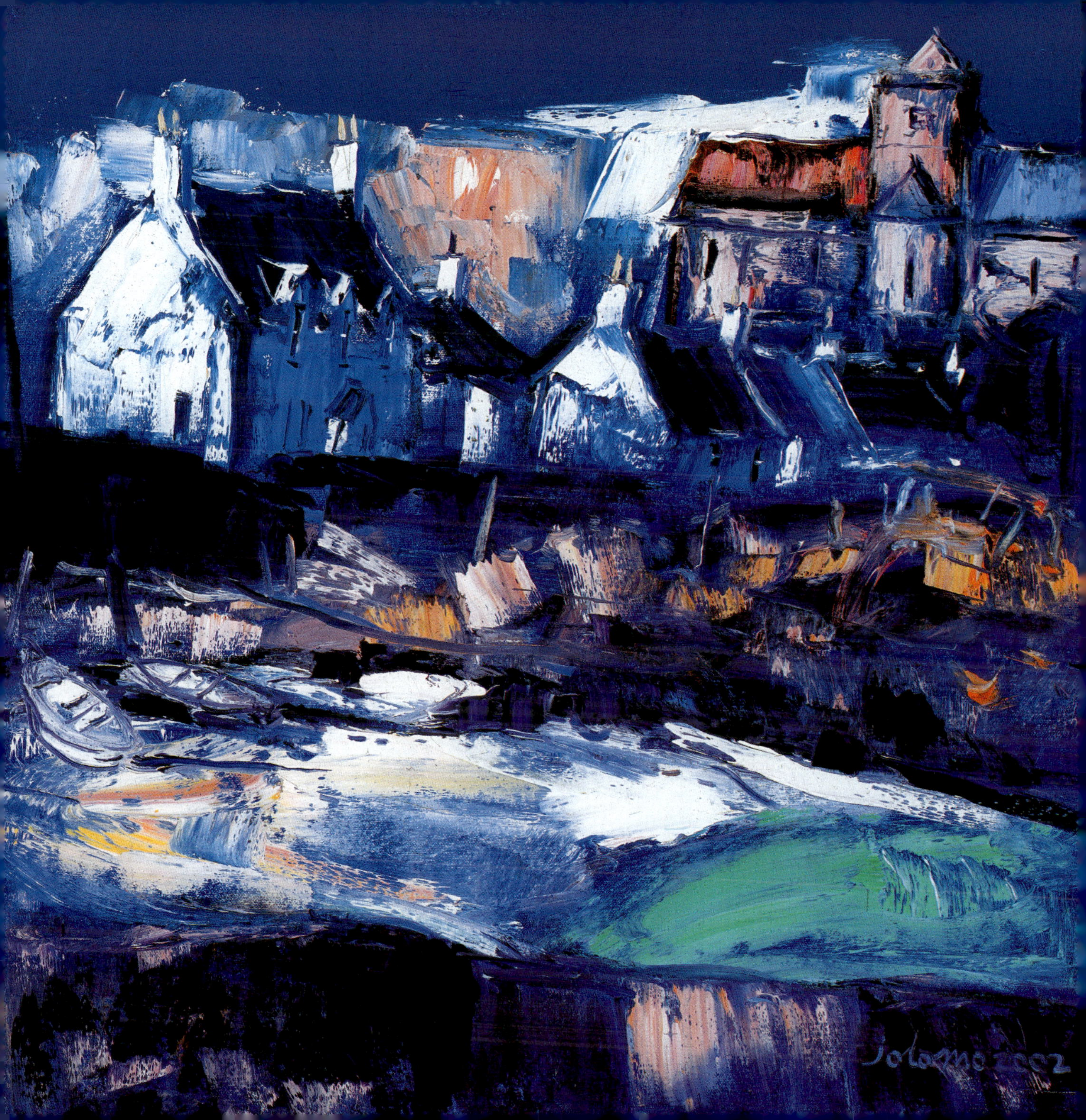

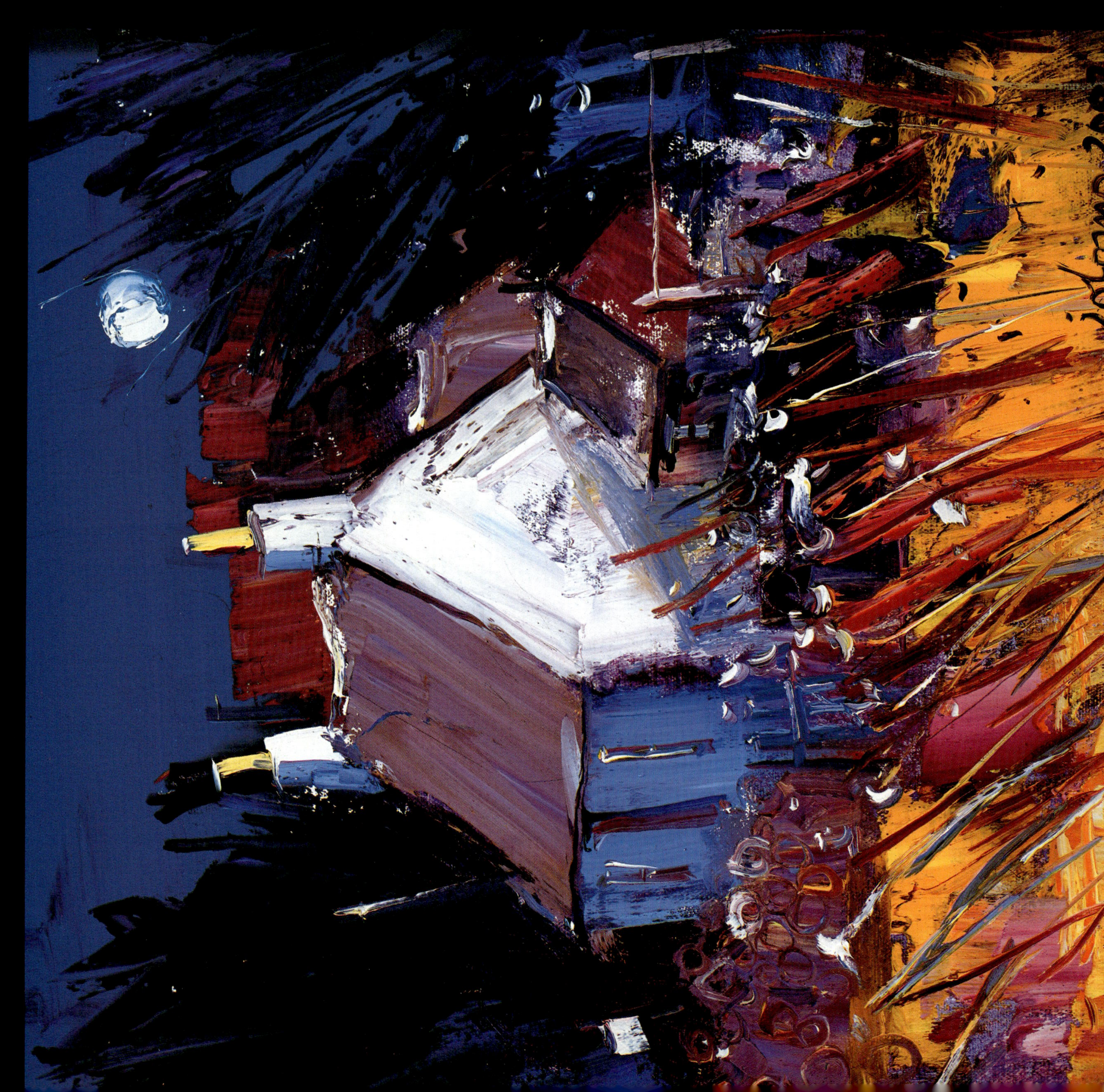

jolomo 2002

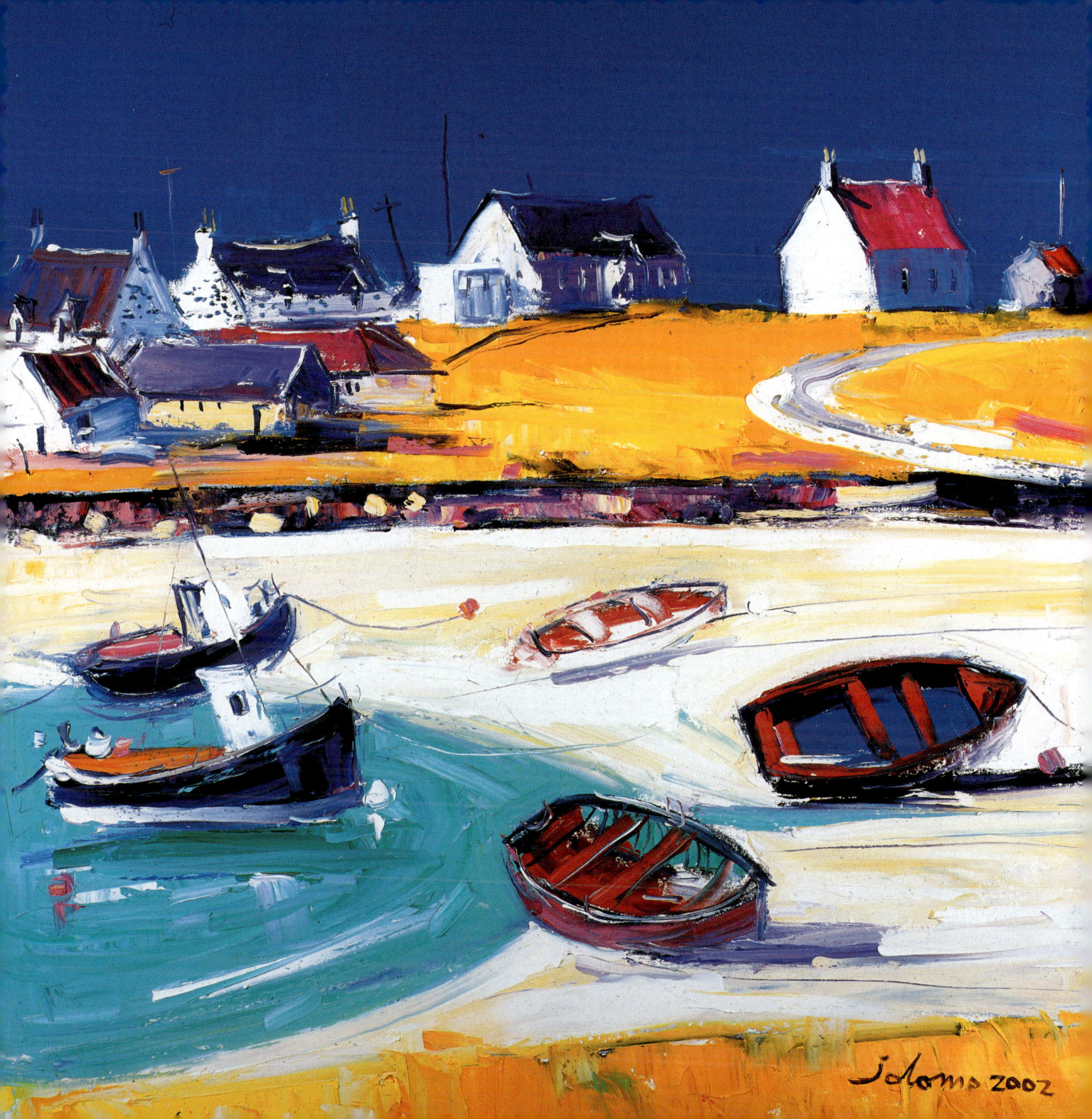

jAdams 2002

John Lowrie Morrison:

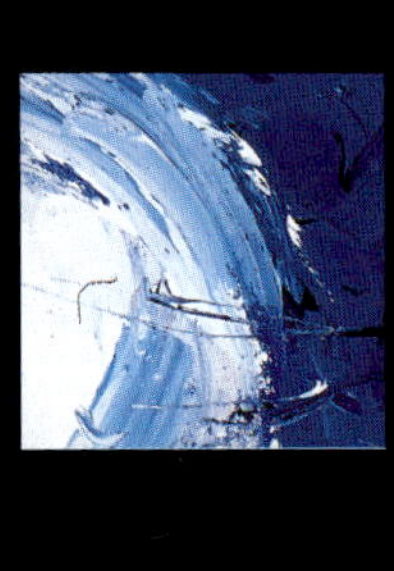

2002

oil

36 x 36"

Genesis 22: 12-14

'Do not lay your hand on the boy or do anything to him; for now I know that you fear God, since you have not withheld your son, your only son, from me'. And Abraham looked up and saw a ram, caught in a thicket by its horns. Abraham went and took the ram and offered it up as a burnt-offering instead of his son. So Abraham called that place 'The Lord will provide'; as it is said to this day, 'On the mount of the Lord it shall be provided.'

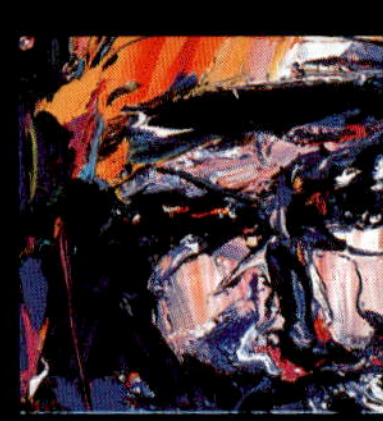

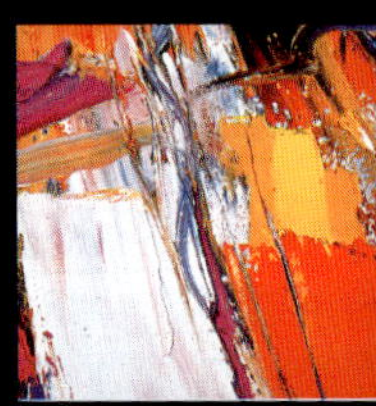

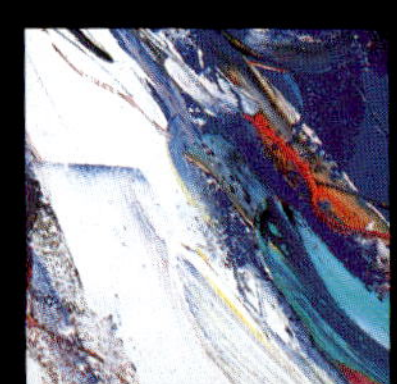

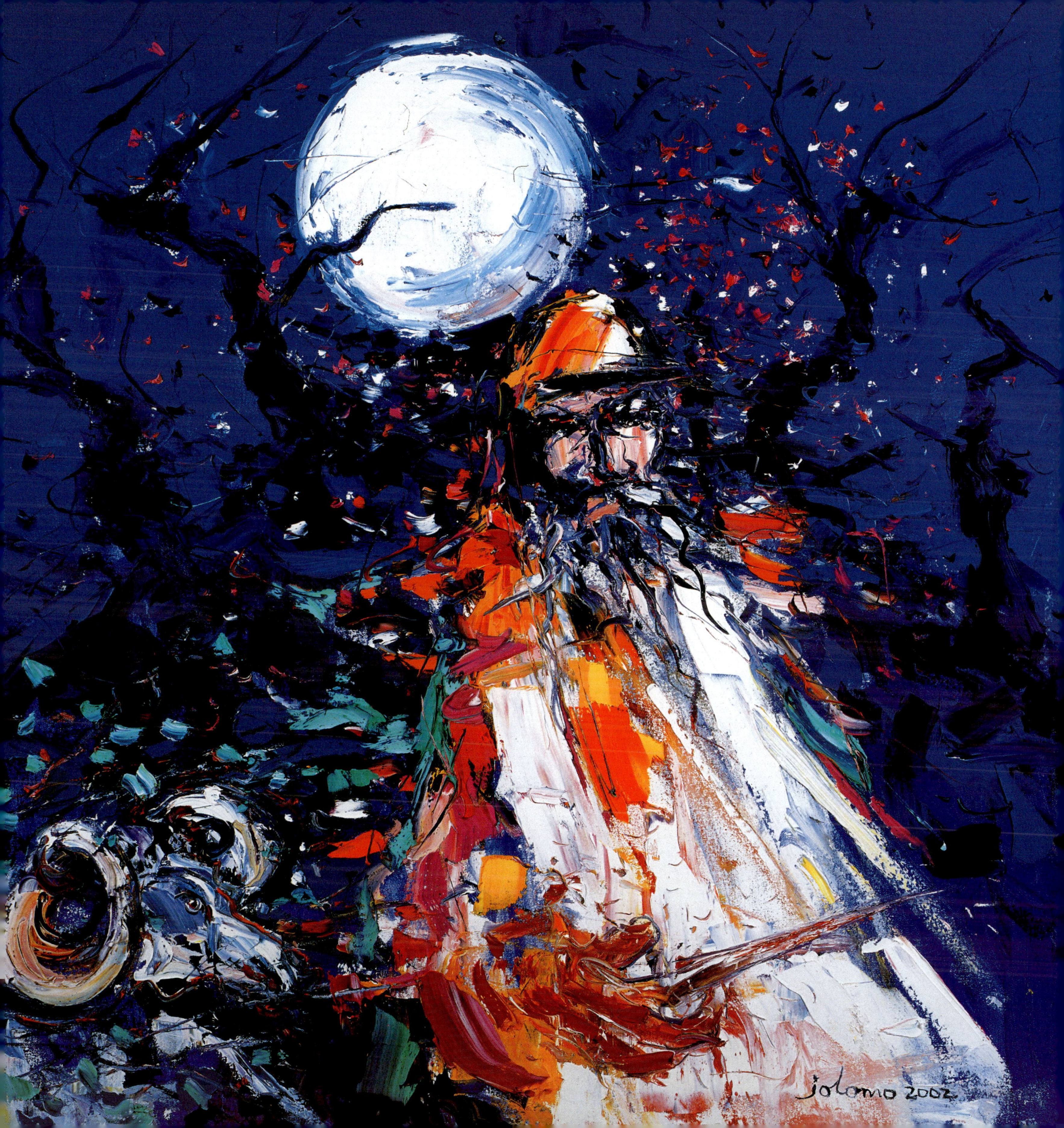

jolomo 2002

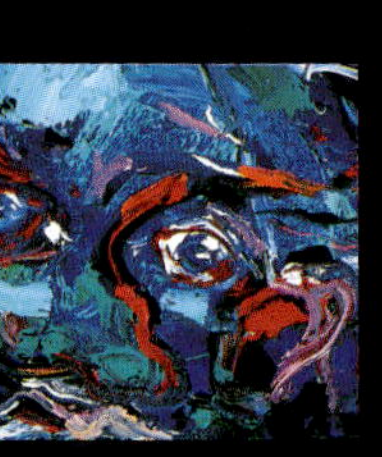

2002

oil

36 x 36”

Luke 8: 27-29

As [Jesus] stepped out on land, a man of the city who had demons met him. For a long time, he had worn no clothes and he did not live in a house but in the tombs. When he saw Jesus, he fell down before him and shouted at the top of his voice, 'What have you to do with me, Jesus, Son of the Most High God? I beg you, do not torment me' - for Jesus had commanded the unclean spirit to come out of the man.

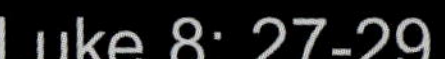

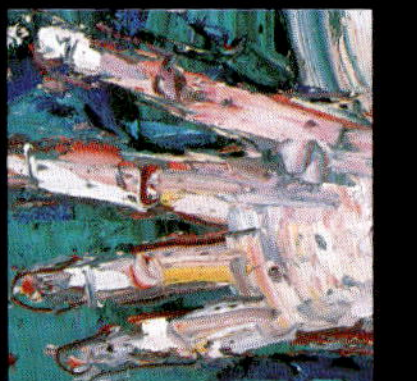

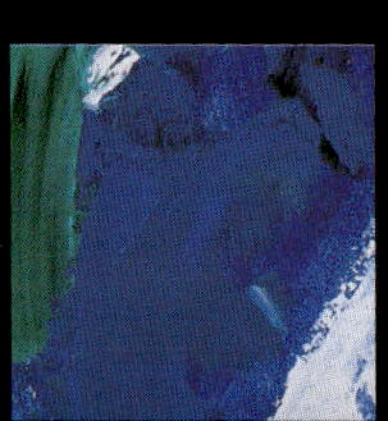

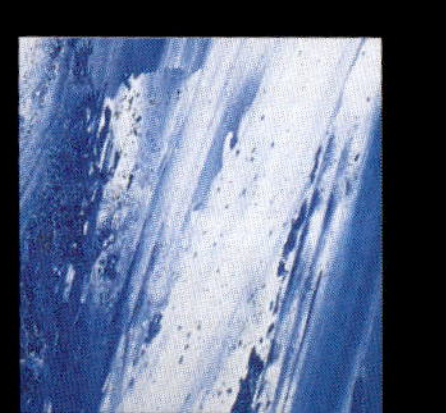

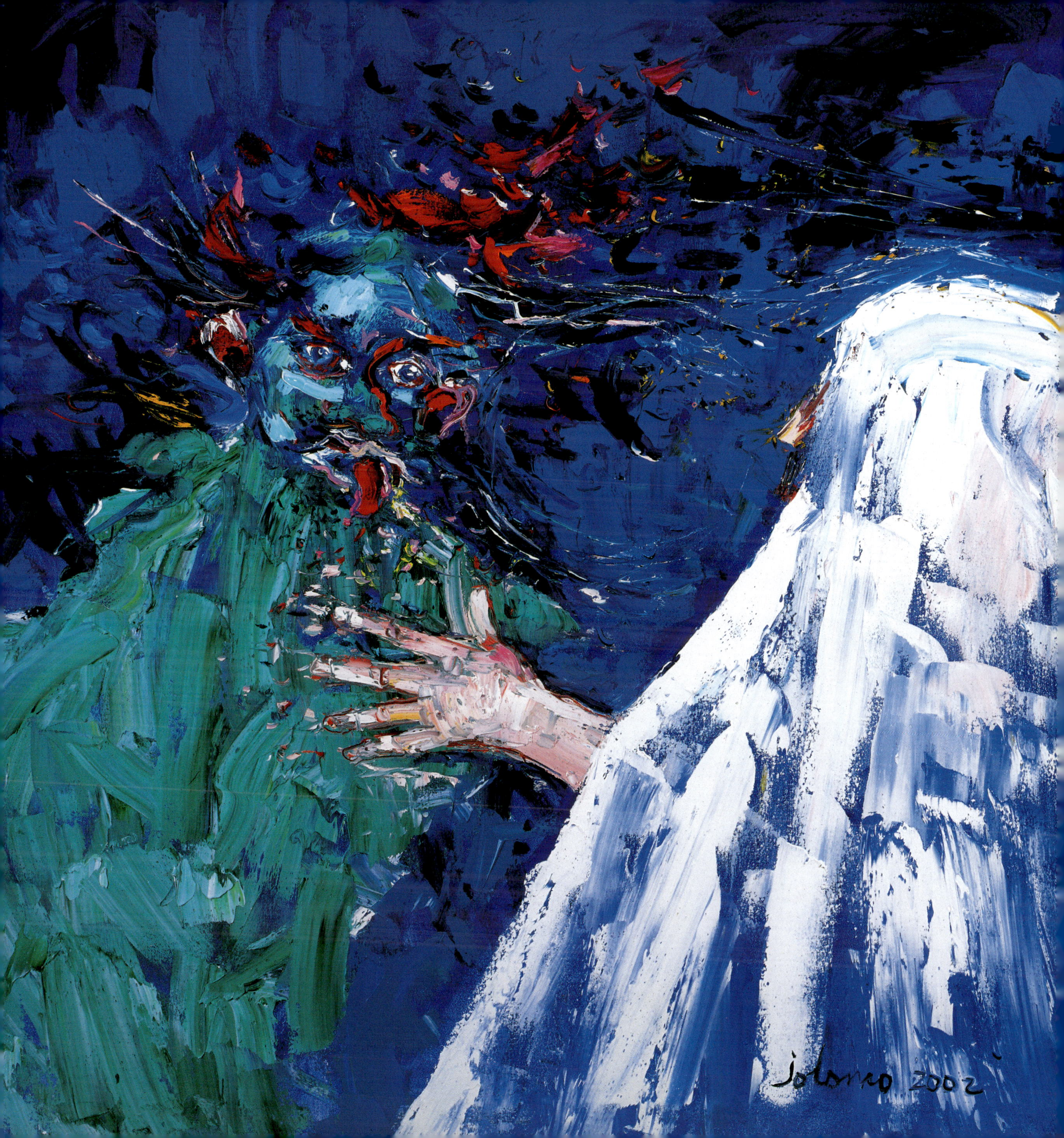

jolomo 2002

John Lowrie Morrison:

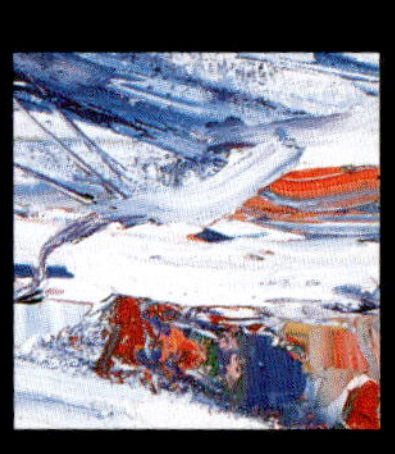

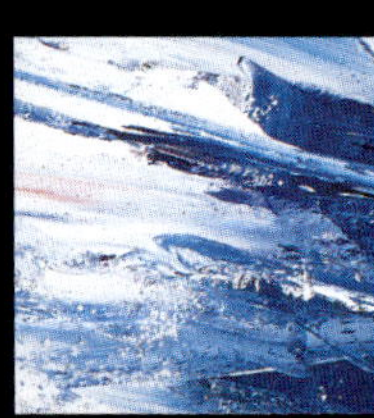

2002

oil

36 x 36''

John 11: 41-44

…Jesus looked upwards and said: 'Father, I thank you for having heard me. I knew that you always hear me, but I have said this for the sake of the crowd standing here, so that they may believe that you sent me'. When he had said this, he cried with a loud voice, 'Lazarus, come out!' The dead man came out, his hands and feet bound with strips of cloth, his face wrapped in a cloth. Jesus said to them, 'Unbind him and let him go'.

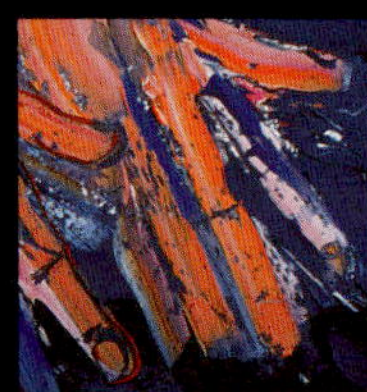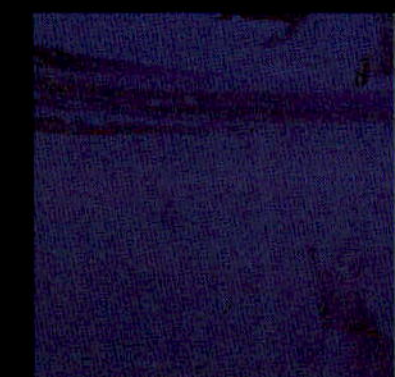

Lazarus, come out!

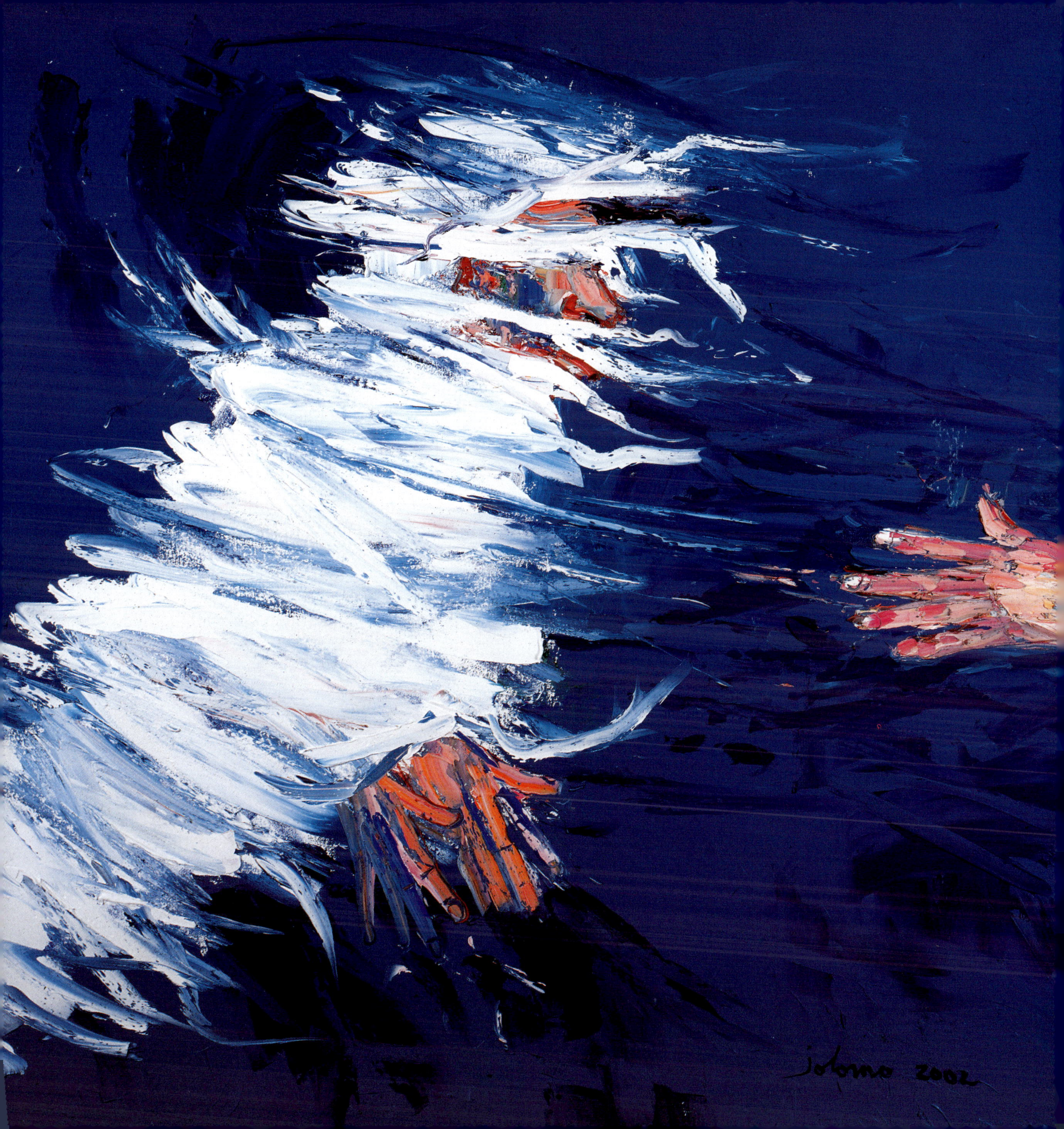

John Lowrie Morrison:

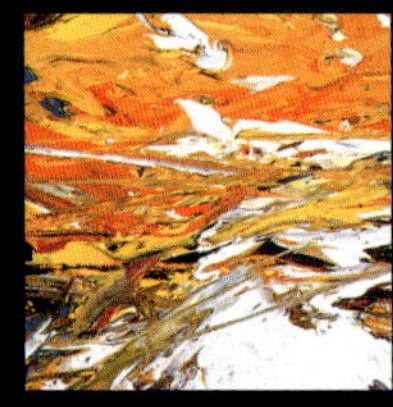

2002

oil

30 x 30''

Mark 14: 35-36

Going a little farther, he threw himself on the ground and prayed that

if it were possible, the hour might pass from him. He said 'Abba, Father,

for you all things are possible; remove this cup from me; yet, not what

I want, but what you want.'

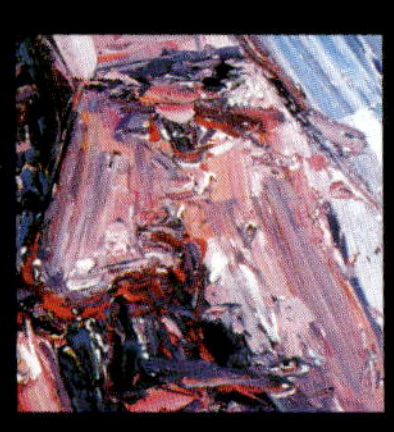

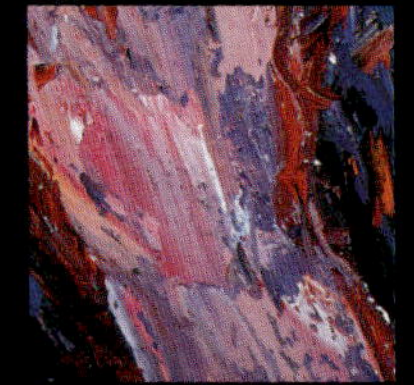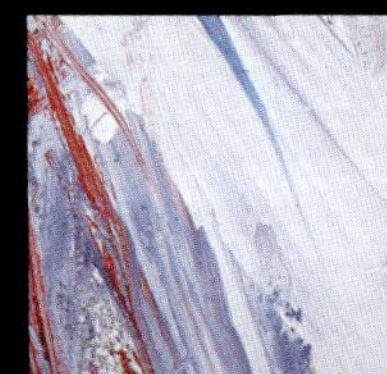

the Colour of life: page 68 & 69

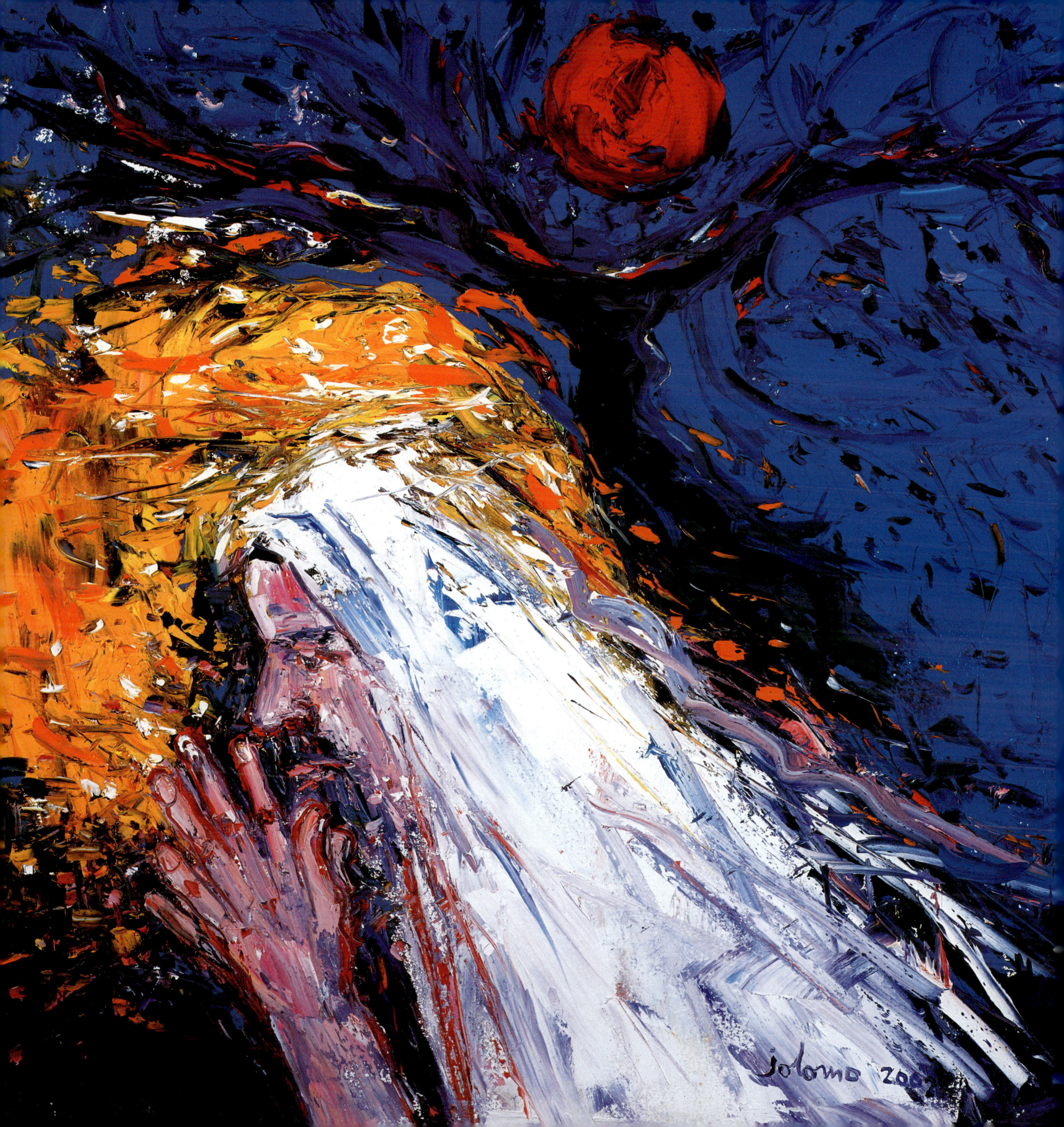

jolomo 2002

John Lowrie Morrison:

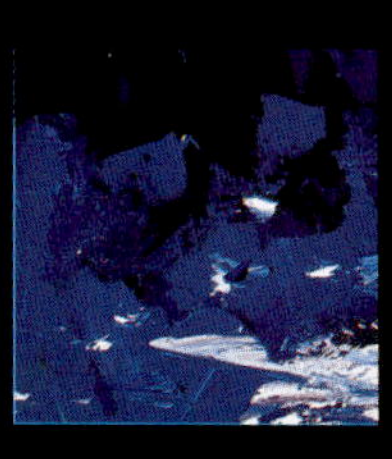

2002

oil

36 x 36"

Matthew 26: 48-51

Now the betrayer had given them a sign, saying, 'The one I will kiss is the man; arrest him.' At once he came up to Jesus and said, 'Greetings, Rabbi!' and kissed him. Jesus said to him, 'Friend, do what you are here to do.' Then they came and laid hands on Jesus and arrested him. Suddenly one of those with Jesus put his hand on his sword, drew it and struck the slave of the high priest, cutting off his ear.

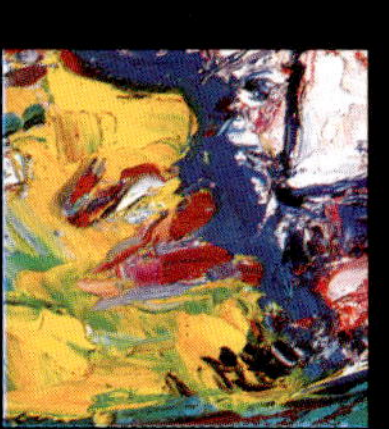

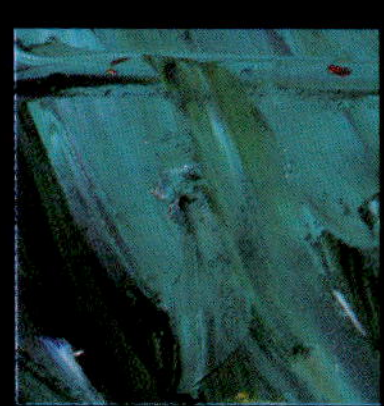

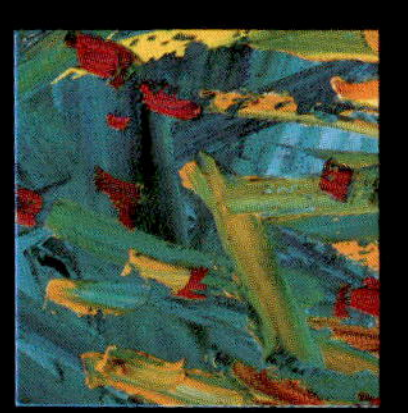

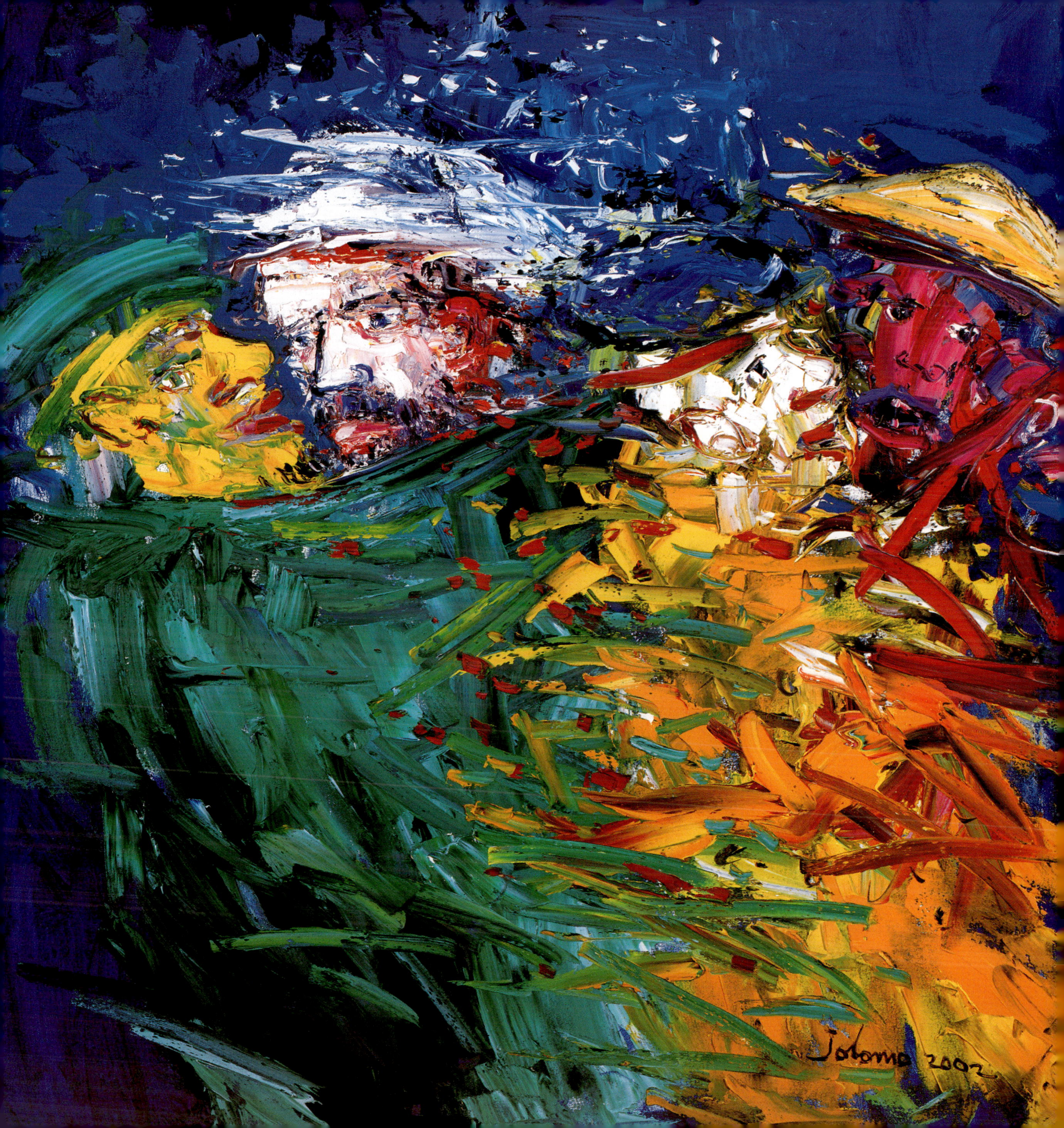

Jolomo 2002

John Lowrie Morrison:

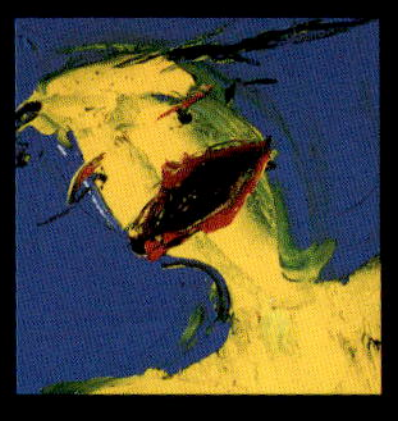

2002

oil

36 x 36''

Matthew 27: 27-31

Then the soldiers of the governor took Jesus away into the governor's headquarters, and they gathered the whole cohort around him. They stripped him and put a scarlet robe on him, and after twisting some thorns into a crown, they put it on his head. They put a reed in his right hand and knelt before him and mocked him, saying, 'Hail, King of the Jews!' They spat on him, and took the reed and struck him on the head. After mocking him, they stripped him of his robe and put his own clothes on him. Then they led him away to crucify him.

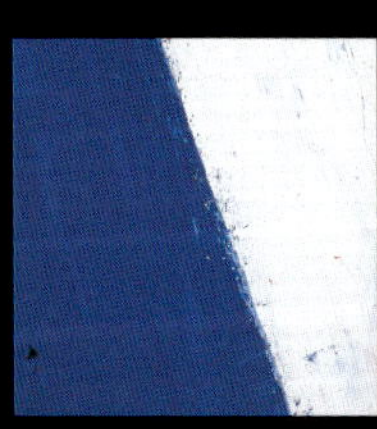

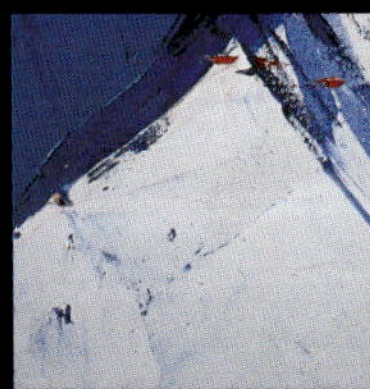

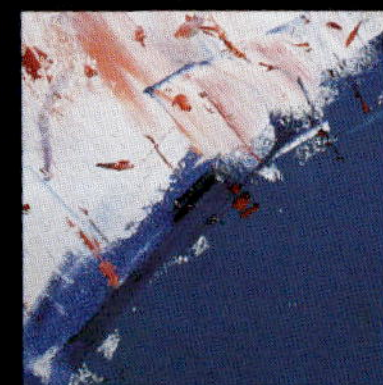

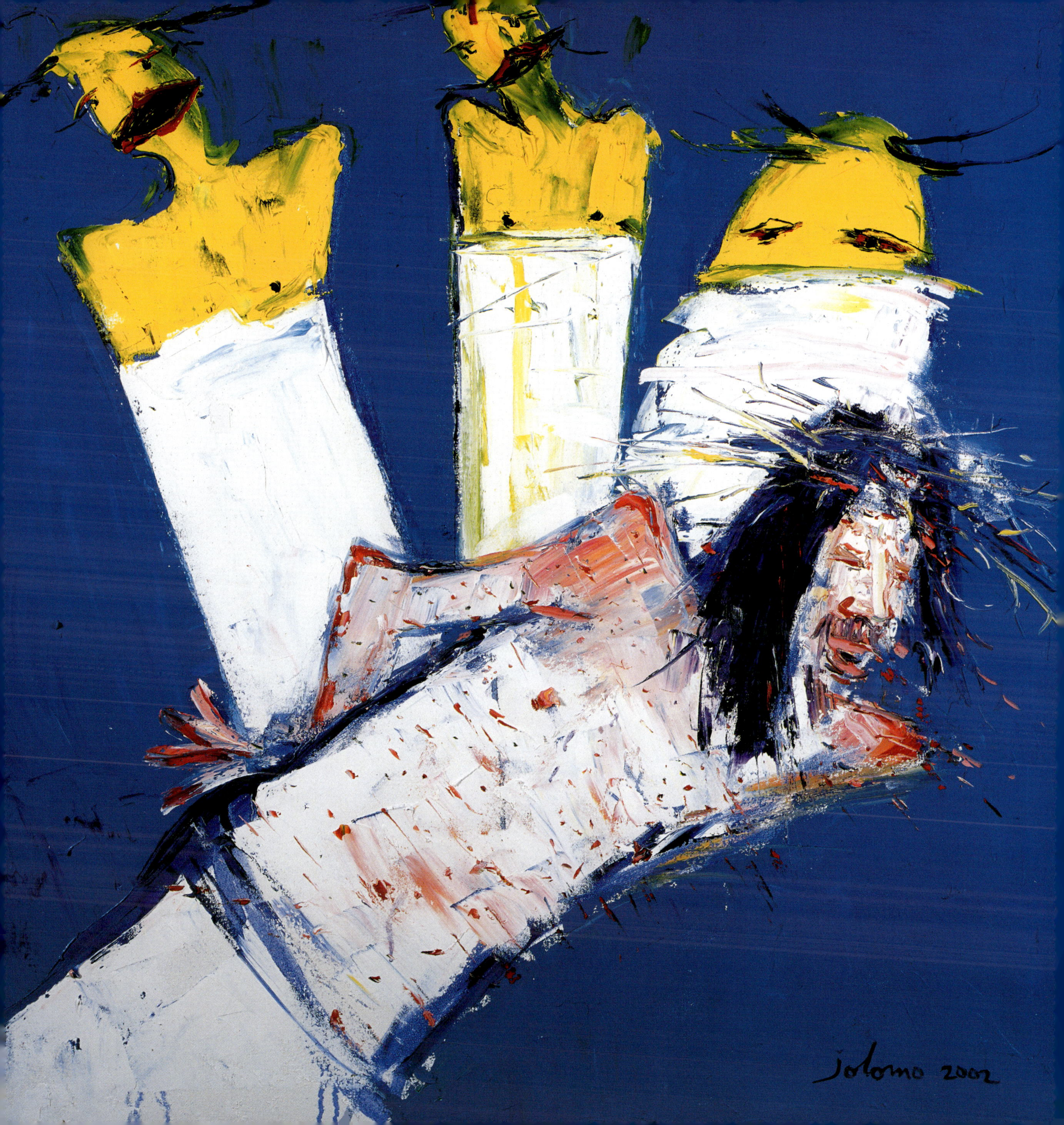

jolomo 2002

John Lowrie Morrison:

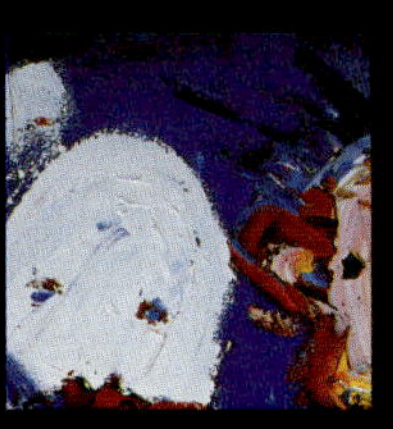

2002

oil

60 x 60"

Luke 23: 26-27

As they led him away, they seized a man, Simon of Cyrene, who was

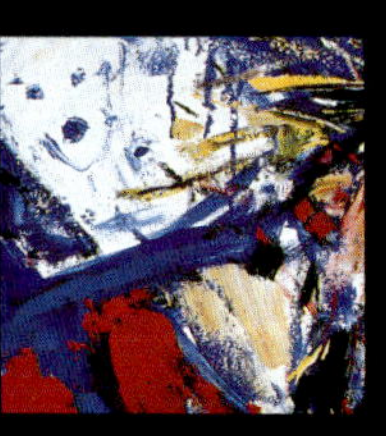

coming from the country, and they laid the cross on him and made him

carry it behind Jesus. A great number of the people followed him, and

among them were women who were beating their breasts and wailing

for him.

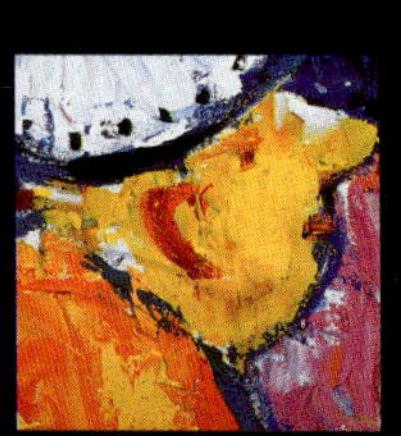
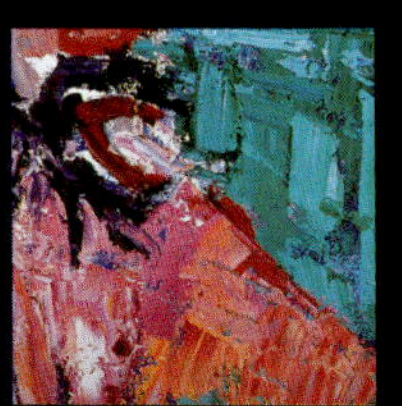

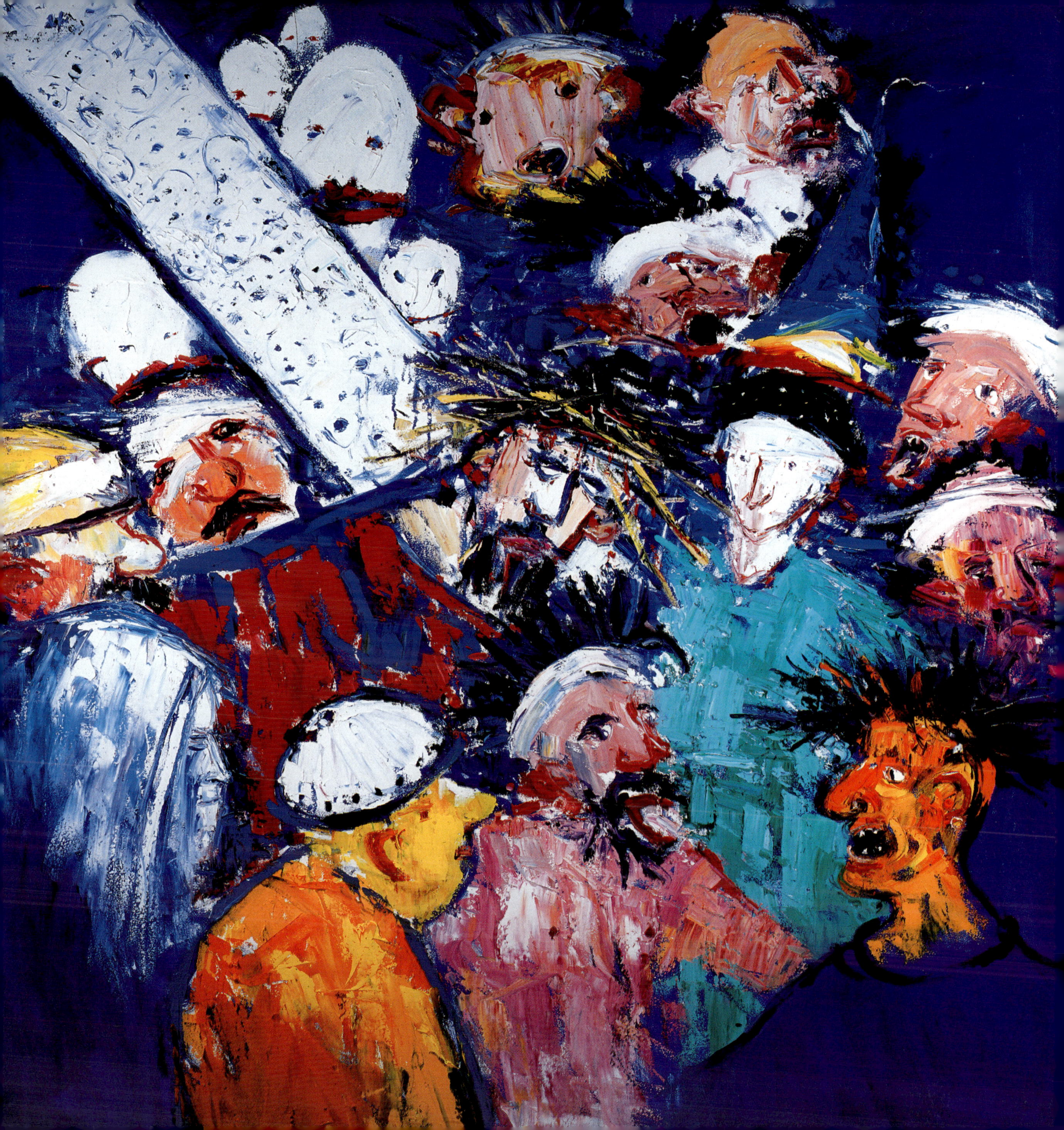

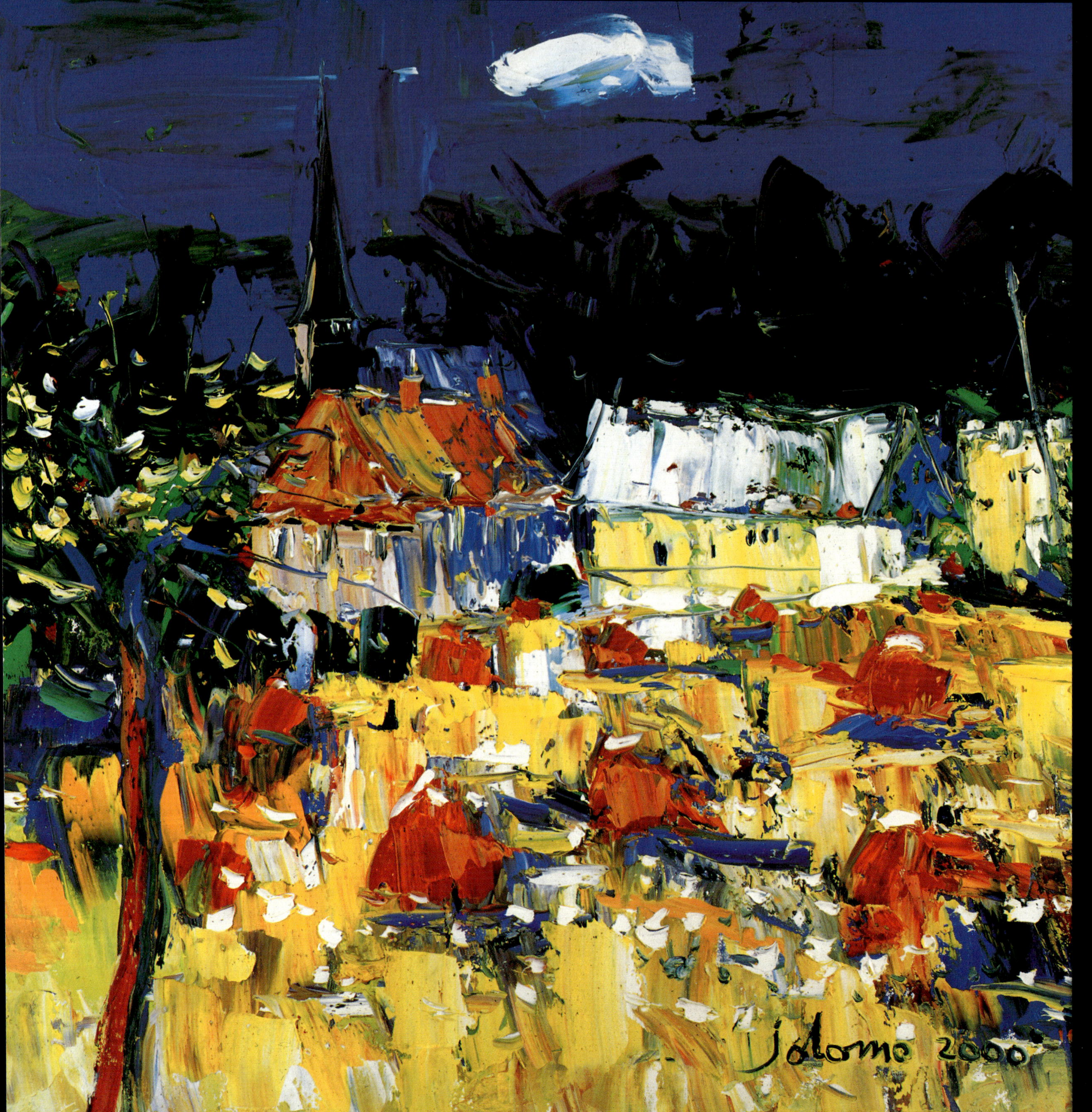

jolomo 2000